MORE

WASHINGTOONS ®

By Mark Alan Stamaty

Prentice Hall Press

New York

Published by Prentice Hall Press
A Division of Simon & Schuster, Inc.
Gulf + Western Building
One Gulf + Western Plaza
New York, New York 10023

PRENTICE HALL PRESS is a trademark of Simon & Schuster, Inc.

Cartoons in this book were originally published in *The Village Voice*

Library of Congress Cataloging-in-Publication Data

Stamaty, Mark Alan.
    More Washingtoons.

    1. United States—Politics and government—
1981–   —Caricatures and cartoons. 2. American
wit and humor, Pictorial. I. Title.
E876.S73   1986   320.973'0207   86-12362
ISBN 0-13-601154-3

Manufactured in the United States of America
10   9   8   7   6   5   4   3   2   1

First Edition

For the Memory of
My (Cartoonist) Father,
Stan Stamaty

© *Stan Stamaty*

SOMETIMES IT SEEMED AS IF THE WHOLE COUNTRY WAS EATING RIGHT OUT OF HIS HAND.

U.S.A.

'Attaway, pooch!

ARF! ARF!

VOTER CHOW — CHUNKS OF TASTY RHETORIC

CAMERAS LOVED HIM.

HE'S SO WARM!

HE KNOWS EXACTLY HOW TO TALK TO ME!

OOOH! MY LENS IS MELTING!!

©1984 maa

HE HAD A SIMILAR EFFECT ON VIEWERS.

MY BRAIN IS MELTING!

SO IS MINE. ...BUT SOMEHOW ...I SEEM TO REMEMBER...

...WASN'T THERE SOME PLACE CALLED..."CENTRAL AMERICA"?... AND ISN'T HE SUPPORTING SOME UNPOPULAR ARMY IN A SECRET WAR?...

IF HE IS, IT MUST BE A VERY NICE WAR!

...RELAX! FORGET ABOUT IT!

I'M TRYING TO! ...BUT WASN'T THERE SOME PLACE CALLED"LEBANON," AND SOMETHING CALLED A "COLD WAR" AND AN "ARMS RACE," AND A "FEDERAL DEFICIT," AND A "TRADE DEFICIT"..?

STOP IT! YOU'RE SPOILING EVERYTHING! ...

DON'T YOU REALIZE THIS PRESIDENT IS TRYING TO MAKE YOU HAPPY?!

IT DOESN'T MATTER WHAT HIS POSITIONS ARE! HE SHIFTS AROUND ALL THE TIME! WHAT MATTERS IS LETTING GO, SURRENDERING TO THE FLOW OF HIS PERSONAL WARMTH! ...AND FORGETTING.

I'M TRYING! I'M TRYING!

...AMERICA IS BACK! AMERICA IS GREAT! AMERICA IS PROUD! ...

YOU KNOW WHO HE REMINDS ME OF?...THERE WAS SOME GUY ABOUT FOUR YEARS AGO WHO USED TO SAY HE COULD BALANCE THE FEDERAL BUDGET BY 1984...

SHUT UP!!

THERE'S PROBABLY NO GREATER THRILL FOR VISITORS TO **D.C. LAND** THAN MEETING THEIR FAVORITE TELEVISION CHARACTERS.

OH WOW! LOOK! IT'S "MR. PRESIDENT"!

HI, MR. PRESIDENT!

HI, KIDS!...

© 1984 M.A.S.

I WANT TO TAKE YOU FOR A RIDE!

OH BOY!!

THE NEXT THING THEY KNEW THEY WERE SEATED ON THE AMAZING **RHETORAIL**, A FUTURISTIC VEHICLE POWERED ENTIRELY BY POLITICAL RHETORIC.

THIS MICROPHONE IS DIRECTLY CONNECTED TO THE ENGINE.

AMERICA IS BACK!

SAID MR. PRESIDENT AND THE RHETORAIL STARTED TO MOVE.

MR. PRESIDENT HAD A VISION OF AMERICA.

THIS IS AMERICA...

...EVERYONE IS PRESIDENT!... EVERYONE IS A FORMER MOVIE STAR!... EVERYONE HAS THEIR OWN RANCH!...

HIS OPTIMISM WAS IRREPRESSIBLE.

CONGRESSMAN BOB FOREHEAD, ON THE OTHER HAND, WAS LESS CONSISTENT.

SNAP OUT OF IT, BOB!

(GROAN)

IS IT A CHARACTER DEFECT TO BURNOUT ON PATÉ IMPORT QUOTAS AFTER TWO AND A HALF MONTHS?

BOB, THIS IS A BIG ONE. THESE PEOPLE ARE...

I KNOW...

... THE NATIONAL ASSOCIATION OF COCKTAIL PARTY GUESTS IS ONE OF **THE** MOST POWERFUL LOBBIES IN WASHINGTON. IF I WIN THIS ONE FOR THEM, MY FUTURE IS SECURE.

BOB'S RETURN TO THAT COMMITTEE HEARING, FOR THOSE CLOSE TO HIM, WAS AN EXAMPLE OF GREATNESS THEY WOULD NOT SOON FORGET.

WHAT A MAN!

FOR PEOPLE WITH A SENSE OF HISTORY, MR. PRESIDENT'S POPULARITY AMONG AMERICA'S YOUTH WAS REMINISCENT OF AN EARLIER PHENOMENON.

M-R-P... R-E-S... I-D-E-N-T...

CATHY
BOBBY
SUSIE
JOEY

FOR CONGRESSMAN BOB FOREHEAD, HOWEVER, IT WAS SIMPLY A SOURCE OF ENVY.

HOW DO I **GET** TO THESE KIDS, CHIP?

WELL, YOU COULD LEAD WITH GRENADA...

© 1984 M.A.S.

...JUST AS WE PROVED IN GRENADA THAT **ANYTHING** IS POSSIBLE WITH A BIG ENOUGH ARMY...

GETTMORE COLLEGE

...SO TOO CAN WE PROVE IN OUR ECONOMY THAT THAT **ANY** LEVEL OF PROSPERITY IS ACHIEVABLE IF WE'RE WILLING TO CUT ENOUGH TAXES.

WE HEAR A LOT OF TALK THESE DAYS ABOUT THE SO-CALLED "DEFICIT." BUT LET ME ASK YOU THIS: HAVE YOU EVER **SEEN** THE DEFICIT?

CAN YOU **FEEL** IT?

IF THERE ACTUALLY **IS** SUCH A THING, **WHERE** DO YOU THINK IT IS?!

I'LL **TELL** YOU WHERE:

IT EXISTS IN THE **MINDS** OF THE NEGATIVISTS AND THE FEAR-MONGERS LIKE MY OPPONENT.

...AND THAT'S WHERE IT SHOULD **STAY!**

A VOTE FOR ME IS A VOTE FOR SOMETHING TANGIBLE:

MONEY IN YOUR POCKETS!

THE APPLAUSE WAS DEAFENING. BOB HAD CROSSED THE GENERATION GAP, AND TOUCHED A SPECIAL PLACE IN THE HEARTS OF AMERICA'S YOUTH.

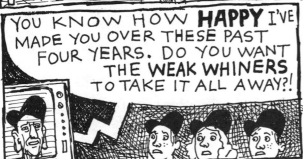

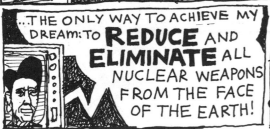

NO ONE WAS QUITE SURE WHERE IT CAME FROM,

PERCEPCIONES IDIOTICAS EN SPORTE DE POLITICAS

© 1984 m.a.s.

...BUT MANY POLITICIANS HAD ENGLISH TRANSLATIONS OF THIS MANUAL, INSTRUCTING THEM IN MEDIA CONTROL, CHARACTER ASSASSINATION,...

..."IT IS POSSIBLE TO **NEUTRALIZE** THE REASONING POWER OF THE VOTERS AND REPLACE IT WITH MINDLESS EMOTION."

...AND THE USE OF **TERROR**:

MY OPPONENT'S POLICIES WILL LEAD YOU TO FINANCIAL **RUIN!!**

AMID SO MUCH NEGATIVITY, THERE WERE STILL SOME PEOPLE WORKING TO MAKE A POSITIVE CONTRIBUTION.

I LOVE THIS WORK...

☙ THE ❧ PERQUISITE FOUNDATION

...FEW PEOPLE REALIZE THE CRUCIAL ROLE OF PERQUISITES TO OUR SURVIVAL AS A NATION.

THEY TAKE FOR GRANTED THE CONTINUED FUNCTIONING OF OUR GOVERNMENT,

...Little REALIZING THAT THE SURVIVAL OF OUR SOCIETY IS THOROUGHLY DEPENDENT ON THE PRESERVATION and ENHANCEMENT OF THE DELICATE AND HIGHLY-COMPLEX **EGO SYSTEM** ROOTED HERE in WASHINGTON D.C.

PERQUISITES PROVIDE ESSENTIAL NOURISH-MENT TO MAINTAIN THE NECESSARY EGOLOGICAL IMBALANCE.

NATURE IS SO INCREDIBLE.

NO DOUBT ABOUT IT: IT WAS AN EXCITING TIME TO BE A TAXPAYER!

©1984 m.a.s.

THE TOP TAX DESIGNERS OF WASHINGTON WERE UNVEILING A BOLD, NEW SPRING COLLECTION, capturing the IMAGINATIONS OF many TAXPAYERS.

I love the simplicity!

AND the REVENUE-NEUTRALITY!

1040 = 1987

I CAN HARDLY WAIT 'TIL APRIL 15th!

BUT SOME WERE less ENTHRALLED.

Maybe I'm OLD-FASHIONED, BUT, without my DEDUCTIONS, I'm AFRAID I'D FEEL EXPOSED!

WITHOUT FREQUENT MEDIA COVERAGE, Congressman BOB FOREHEAD FELT HALF-ALIVE.

...ISH...
...YOU...
...ISH...

...YOU...

WHAT'S HE SAYING?

"ISSUE."...

HE NEEDS AN ISSUE ...TO GET HIM SOME COVERAGE.

HOW ABOUT TAX SIMPLIFICATION? LET'S GIVE HIM ONE OF THOSE TAX PLANS.

GOOD IDEA! ...IF WE CAN COME UP WITH THE RIGHT ADJECTIVE. "FAIR","FAST," AND "FLAT" ARE ALREADY TAKEN.

FOR SEVERAL DAYS, THEY BURIED THEMSELVES IN THE DICTIONARY.

...FAT TAX? FIRM TAX? FOUL TAX? FOOL TAX?...

FAKE TAX? FISHY TAX? FLEE TAX? FLAW TAX?

FINALLY, THEY CHOSE ONE.

THE FUN TAX!

AND BOB ANNOUNCED IT.

...YOU SIMPLY WRITE IN THE AMOUNT OF TAX IT WOULD BE FUN FOR YOU TO PAY AND SIGN YOUR NAME.

IF EVERYONE WRITES IN A ZERO, THEN OUR ECONOMY WILL ACHIEVE ITS MAXIMUM GROWTH RATE AT LAST!

SHRIEKED THE SPIRIT OF SUPPLY SIDE THROUGH THIS DEVOTED MEDIUM.

ONE RESPONSIBILITY OF A CONGRESSMAN IS TO KEEP HIS *constituents* INFORMED ABOUT WHAT'S GOING ON *in WASHINGTON.*

CAPITOL HILL REPORT FROM CONGRESSMAN BOB FOREHEAD

FOREHEAD LEADS FIGHT FOR A "BETTER AMERICA"

FOREHEAD DEFENDS TAXPAYERS

CONGRESSMAN FOREHEAD SPEAKS OUT AGAINST SOVIET TYRANNY

SOCIAL SECURITY CALLED "SACRED" BY BOB FOREHEAD

FOREHEAD SCORNS CONGRESSIONAL INEFFICIENCY

FOREHEAD PRAISES WOMEN AND MEN

FOREHEAD FAVORS PROSPERITY

FOREHEAD CALLS FOR WORLD PEACE

©1984 m.a.s.

ANOTHER RESPONSIBILITY IS TO SERVE HIS CONSTITUENTS IN A WIDE VARIETY OF WAYS.

NO, MOMMY! NO, DADDY! I DON'T **WANT** YOU TO READ ME A STORY!...

THE THREE OCELOTS

...I WANT **CONGRESSMAN FOREHEAD** TO READ ME A STORY!

ALL RIGHT, DEAR! ALL RIGHT!

...WE FLEW IN LAST NIGHT! YOU'VE GOT TO HELP US! HE WON'T GO TO SLEEP UNTIL YOU READ HIM A STORY!

WAAAH!

AGAIN?

BECAUSE OF THAT, BOB WAS LATE FOR HIS APPOINTMENT WITH GERARD OXBOGGLE, CHAIRMAN OF THE GLOMINOID CORPORATION.

IT'S TOO MUCH!... I CAN'T BEAR IT!

MR. OXBOGGLE, WHAT'S WRONG?!

I'VE HAD IT! I REALLY HAVE!..

THERE'S AN ARTICLE IN THE PAPER TODAY ATTACKING GLOMINOID FOR GROSSING FOURTEEN BILLION DOLLARS WHILE PAYING "ONLY," IT SAYS, 270 DOLLARS IN TAXES.

.."ONLY" 270 DOLLARS, EH? WHAT ABOUT COMPANIES THAT PAID **NONE AT ALL**?! WHY DO THEY PICK ON **US**?!...

IT WAS TIMES LIKE THIS WHEN BOB REALIZED THE DEEPER VALUE OF HIS WORK.

MR. OXBOGGLE, WHEN MY "FUN TAX" PASSES, YOUR SUFFERING WILL BE OVER!...

Sabotage Patch Doll

HE COULD *hardly* CONTAIN HIS EXCITEMENT.

IT'S A WINNER! I can FEEL IT. Wait'll you see...

SAID THE PRESIDENT OF THE FLIPDIP TOY CO.

ONE OF *the* DESIGNERS Demonstrated.

THE SABOTAGE PATCH DOLL

ON THE SURFACE, it's A CUTE, CUDDLY COMPANION, GOOD FOR HOURS OF WHOLESOME PLAY...

© 1984 m.a.s.

BUT ONE QUICK YANK ON ITS HAIR REVEALS AN AUTOMATIC ANTI-PERSONNEL ROCKET LAUNCHER.

IN another simple MANEUVER,...

...THE DOLL FOLDS INSIDE OUT, TRANSFORMING *into* A MOBILE, HIGH-PERFORMANCE NUCLEAR WEAPONS SYSTEM READY FOR SUSTAINED COMBAT!

IT'S ONE OF *the* MOST VERSATILE TOYS EVER MADE!

...WHICH WAS HOW CONGRESSMAN FOREHEAD *Sometimes* FELT.

QUICK, BOB, YOU'RE LATE! GET OUT THERE!

I FEEL LIKE A BASKETBALL.

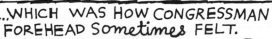

BUT HE LET HIS STAFF KEEP DRIBBLING HIM AND TOSSING HIM,...

CITIZENS FOR MORE MONEY ANNUAL LUNCHEON

WE MUST GET GOVERNMENT OUT OF GOVERNMENT.

...ALL THE WHILE HARBORING A HALF-CONSCIOUS, LIFE-LONG DREAM.

SOMEDAY ALL THE TOYS WILL BE MINE!

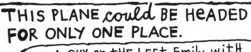

THIS PLANE *could* BE HEADED FOR ONLY ONE PLACE.

...THat GUY ON THE LEFT, Emily, WITH THE BRIEFCASE, He USED TO BE SECRETARY OF DEFENSE,...and over ON THE RIGHT SIDE iS SENATOR SUEDE,...and BEHIND Him iS CONGRESSMAN GORGLER...

IT WAS MORE *than* JUST Famous PEOPLE. THERE WAS SOMETHING IN THE ATMOSPHERE, SOME-*thing* IN THE EYES OF *the* PASSENGERS ON *the* WASHINGTON SHUTTLE. LIKE A FORCE, PULLING *them*.

©1985 m.a.s.

THEY SET UP PORTABLE OFFICES IN THEIR SEATS AND *went about* DECIDING VARIOUS PORTIONS OF *the* FATE OF *the* WORLD.

The Effect OF Fall-out on Carrots

FARM POLICY DURING NUCLEAR WAR

YOU COULD FEEL IT IN THE WAY THEY READ *their* NEWS-PAPERS...

PRESIDENT THROWS SNOWBALL GRANTS PHOTO OPP.

...QUICKLY, HUNGRILY.

WHAT iS IT ABOUT THESE PEOPLE, GEORGE?

IT'S CALLED THE "INSIDE THE BELTWAY MENTALITY." THE BELTWAY AROUND WASHINGTON EMITS A A MAGNETIC FIELD THAT CAN ALTER THE SIZE AND SHAPE OF BRAIN CELLS.

THIS CAUSES A PERCEPTUAL MAGNIFICATION OF ONESELF AND ALL SURROUNDINGS WITHIN THE MAGNETIC. FIELD.

Meanwhile, in A RESTAURANT WITHIN THE MAGNETIC FIELD, TWO CONGRESSMEN ATE LUNCH.

YOU SEEM WORRIED, BOB.

LAST NIGHT, I HAD A TERRIBLE NIGHTMARE

...I DREAMED I WAS NO LONGER LARGER-THAN-LIFE. I HAD TO WALK AROUND BEING THE SAME SIZE AS LIFE.

AND THEN I STARTED TO SHRINK...

I'VE HAD THAT, BOB. DELIVER A COUPLE OF HISTORIC ADDRESSES AND YOU'LL FEEL MUCH BETTER!

IT WAS A GROWING MOVEMENT.

THE RECENT PERIOD BETWEEN THE ELECTION AND THE INAUGUR-ATION, A PERIOD OF RELATIVE CALM AND STABILITY, HAS DEMONSTRATED THE **EFFECTIVENESS** OF **GOVERNMENTAL INACTION!**

SAID THE Executive DIRECTOR OF "CITIZENS FOR GOVERNMENTAL INACTION."

© 1985 M.A.S.

THIS IS NOT to SAY, However, that WE SEE NO USEFUL ROLE IN PUBLIC LIFE FOR ELECTED OFFICIALS. Quite to THE CONTRARY.

WE **ENCOURAGE** LIVELY DEBATE ON RADIO AND TV TALK SHOWS, WHERE ALL POSSIBLE COURSES OF ACTION CAN BE THOROUGHLY DISCUSSED. WE FIRMLY ENDORSE **PERPETUAL** CONSIDERATION OF MX and "STAR WARS" DEPLOYMENT AND **STRONGLY** SUPPORT "**TAKING A LOOK AT**" ALL MANNER OF CUTS IN FEDERAL SPENDING SO LONG AS NONE OF THESE POLICIES ARE ACTUALLY IMPLEMENTED!

THEIR VIEWPOINT GAVE TALK SHOWS SOMETHING TO TALK ABOUT.

YOU SEEM TO BE ADVOCATING A KIND OF GOVERNMENT-BY-TALK-SHOWS.

VERY DEFINITELY.

THEIR POLITICAL ACTION COMMITTEE GAVE CONGRESSMAN FOREHEAD $5,000.

I'M SORRY. I CAN'T ACCEPT IT.

WHAT?!!

I CAN'T BELIEVE THIS, BOB! YOUR IMAGE ON TELEVISION IS EVERYTHING YOU'VE EVER LIVED FOR!

TAKE ANOTHER LOOK...

TAKE A LOOK AT A MAN WHO BELIEVES IN THE "DUMPING RIGHTS ACT" AND THE "FUN TAX" AND THE "MOOD MISSILE," AND WILL NOT **REST** UNTIL THOSE BILLS BECOME LAW!

BOB'S AIDE WAS STUNNED.

GOSH, BOB! I'VE NEVER SEEN YOU BE SO... SUBSTANTIVE! ARE YOU O.K?

WELL, ACTUALLY, I THINK I'M GETTING THE FLU. I FEEL FEVERISH...

THAT EXPLAINS IT!

A SLIGHT HUNCHING OF THE SHOULDERS, one HAND inside his jacket, STRAIGHTENING HIS tie. THE MAN KNEW HOW to STRAIGHTEN HIS tie.

HE WAS DOING A POWERFUL JOB OF EVOKING.

EVEN congressman BOB FOREHEAD, chairman OF THE JFK-LOOK-ALIKE CAUCUS, could not EVOKE A JFK aura EQUAL to the current EFFECTIVENESS OF THIS man,...

© 1984 m.a.s.

...WHO WAS RUNNING FOR PRESIDENT.

I WANT TO DISCUSS THE ISSUES!

SO DO I!

...YOU ARE WEAK ON THE NUCLEAR FREEZE!

Said HIS PRINCIPAL OPPONENT. THAT'S NOT TRUE!

YOU WANT TO BUILDDOWN THE FREEZE!

YOU'RE WRONG!...

WHAT I WANT TO DO IS BUILD UP THE FREEZE WHILE FREEZING DOWN THE BUILDUP BY BUILDING THE BUILDUP DOWN!...

...BUT YOU WANT TO FREEZE DOWN THE UPBUILD WITHOUT FIRST BUILDING UP THE BUILDDOWN, WHICH WOULD HAVE THE EFFECT OF BUILDING DOWN THE UPDOWN UP!...

...NOW, ON THE UPSIDE, THAT WOULD DOWNUP THE UPDOWNUP, BUT THE DOWNSIDE IS THAT THE DOWNUP WOULD UPUPDOWN!

NO! DOWN UP UP!

NO! UP DOWN UP!

NO! UP DOWN DOWN!

NO! UPUP DOWN!

NO! DOWN!

the DEBATE CONTINUED and CONTINUED and CONTINUED and CONTINUED...

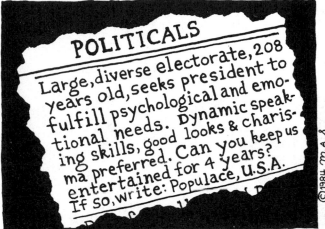

POLITICALS

Large, diverse electorate, 208 years old, seeks president to fulfill psychological and emotional needs. Dynamic speaking skills, good looks & charisma preferred. Can you keep us entertained for 4 years? If so, write: Populace, U.S.A.

©1984 M.A.S.

Hi, I'm BOB FOREHEAD. I'm RUNNING FOR PRESIDENT.

He TRIED NOT TO SHOW IT.

MAYBE THEY WOULDN'T NOTICE THAT HE WAS A SHELL OF HIS FORMER SELF.

HERE, LET ME HELP YOU WITH THOSE GROCERIES...

SOMETIMES A PERSONAL TOUCH COULD WIN THE CANDIDATE A VOTE.

WHO'S THAT SHOVELING THE SNOW ON OUR FRONT WALK?

THAT'S CONGRESSMAN FOREHEAD.

YOU'RE TRYING TOO HARD, BOB.

SAID an ADVISER BACK at THE motel.

I'VE GOT to.

MAYBE IT'S JUST not YOUR YEAR.

IT'S A STRANGE time FOR ME. ...I feel ADRIFT, ...aimless, RUDDERLESS...

BUT MAYBE *if* I WERE PRESIDENT... *maybe* **THAT** WOULD GIVE *me* A SENSE OF... PURPOSE...

...IT'S WORTH A TRY.

WHICH WAS EXACTLY WHAT SEVERAL TV NEWS SHOW STAFFERS SAID as THEY TRIED TO CONTACT A PARTICULAR PRESIDENTIAL ECONOMIC ADVISER.

BUT THEY DIDN'T HAVE MUCH SUCCESS.

RRRRiiiNNGGG!!

ZYX357 Want to chat? URGENT!

Hello. How are you?

I am an economic adviser to the president. I am being held hostage in my office in Washington to prevent me from being interviewed on television. Please help me escape.

Sorry. I live in Provo, Utah. Good luck.

ALL NIGHT LONG He tapped AT the KEYS OF HIS COMPUTER TERMINAL, TRYING tO CONTACT A RESCUER.

© 1984 mark alan alam alam stamaty

HE'S A DANGEROUS MAN!...

SAID ONE DEFENSE CONTRACTOR tO ANOTHER.

HE WANTS TO CUT tHE DEFENSE BUDGET!

THE WORDS INSTILLED A SILENT HORROR.

HE HAD OFFENDED *many* PEOPLE, BUT NONE SO MUCH AS A CERTAIN ECONOMICS JOURNALIST NAMED CRAIG PAUL ED BOB.

All tHINGS ARE POSSIBLE WitH...

CRAIG PAUL ED BOB WAS NO CASUAL OBSERVER OF THE ECONOMICS SCENE, BUT, RATHER, *an* ARDENT DEVOTEE OF A PARTICULAR FAITH:

... SUPPLY SIDE!

and tHERE WAS A STRONG BASIS FOR **CRAIG PAUL ED BOB'S** BELIEF.

I'd ALWAYS SENSED tHAT SUPPLY SIDE WAS tHE ONLY TRUE PATH, BUT tHEN ONE DAY I HAD AN EXPERIENCE tHAT CONVINCED ME BEYOND ANY DOUBT...

IT WAS IN EARLY 1982. HE WAS SEATED at HIS DESK WATCHING A CRITIC OF SUPPLY SIDE ON TV.

...THE TAX CUTS WILL CREATE HUGE DEFICITS AND THE DEFICITS WILL DESTROY US!

THEN, SUDDENLY, *across* tHE ROOM, HE SAW A **VISION.** IT WAS THE FEDERAL DEFICIT APPEARING TO HIM IN HUMAN FORM.

FORGIVE tHEM, MY SON...THEY DO NOT UNDERSTAND MY PURPOSE...

...A TRILLION DOLLARS IN DEFICITS COULD **NEVER** EQUAL THE HARM OF THE SMALLEST TAX HIKE! ...

FROM *THAT* MOMENT ON, CRAIG PAUL ED BOB VOWED TO DEVOTE HIMSELF TO DEFENDING THE DEFICIT.

YOU COULD ALWAYS tELL WHERE HE WAS in THE CROWD, even WHEN YOU couldn't SEE Him.

EVERYBODY wanted to ASK him A QUESTION.

BACK on THE PLANE, he GAVE interviews, and ANSWERED the SAME QUESTIONS AgAiN and AgAiN.

THE answers AND iMAGES WENt OUt THROUGH tHE MEDIA.

It JUST FEELS SO GOOD!

SAID tHE VOTERS...

..AS tHEY RODE tHE MOMENTUM to Electoral EUPHORIA.

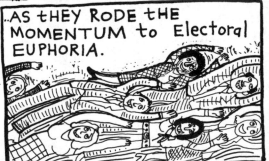

OTHERS HESITATED.

COME ON! JOIN US!

OH, I DON'T KNOW...

AW, LOOSEN UP! IT'S FUN!

ONE PERSON WHO WASN'T HAVING FUN WAS CongresSman BOB FOREHEAD.

YOU'RE FIRED!

He said to His GESTUROGRAPHER.

THAT DAY HE HELD A PRESS CONFERENCE, BUT IT WAS POORLY ATTENDED.

...Do YOU PLAN TO CONTINUE YOUR PRESIDENTIAL CAMPAIGN?

I'M NOT SURE, MA.

FINALLY, HE DROPPED OUT.

...YOU WON't HAVE FOREHEAD TO IGNORE anymore...

...UNTIL NEXT time.

SHE MADE HER FIRST APPEARANCE at THE POLLS at 8:30 A.M. on PRIMARY DAY.

WOULD it BE ALL RIGHT IF I VOTED 40% FOR one CANDIDATE, 35% FOR another, AND 25% FOR THE OTHER?

NO, SHE WAS **told**, SHE WOULD HAVE TO CHOOSE one.

tap, tap, tap, tap, tap, tap,...

The REST OF THE MORNING WAS SPENT at THE TYPEWRITER.

©1984 m.a.s.

At 2:00 P.M., SHE APPEARED at THE POLLS again.

O.K. I'VE DECIDED WHO I'm VOTING FOR, BUT WITH my VOTE I'm INCLUDING A WRITTEN EXPLANATION OF MY DOUBTS AND RESERVATIONS... I'VE MANAGED TO KEEP IT UNDER 20 PAGES...

I'm SORRY, DEAR...

THE REST OF THE AFTERNOON WAS SPENT WALKING THE STREETS, UNDECIDED once AGAIN.

NONE OF THE CANDIDATES TRULY EXPRESSES **ME!**

SHE SAID to the POLL-TAKER WHO NEVER LEFT HER SIDE.

AS SHE WALKED, SHE NOTICED THE SAME TROUBLED EXPRESSION ON MANY FACES. THE STREETS WERE FILLED WITH UNDECIDED VOTERS.

THEN, SUDDENLY, one MEMORY OF A NUANCE OF ONE OF THE CANDIDATES SEEMED TO outWEIGH THE OTHERS.

TAXI! QUICK! GET ME TO THE POLLS BEFORE I CHANGE MY MIND!

THAT IMPULSE and HOW TO INDUCE IT WAS the SUBJECT OF LIFE-LONG STUDY FOR DR. THEOBOLD FRIZZMONT.

THERE IS NO MYSTERY ABOUT IT. IT'S BASIC PSYCHOELECTORALONICS.

MUCH OF DR. FRIZZMONT'S WORK WAS CONTROVERSIAL, BUT CONGRESSMAN FOREHEAD HIRED HIM NONETHELESS.

THE VOTING IMPULSE IS NOTHING MORE THAN A SIMPLE CHEMICAL REACTION,...

...WHICH CAN BE PREDICTABLY INDUCED BY ANYONE WILLING TO LISTEN TO ME...

BOB WAS LISTENING.

It WAS ONE OF *his* BEST *Pitches.*

It LOOKED LIKE A JUICY FASTBALL RIGHT DOWN THE MIDDLE...

WE'VE GOT TO CUT SOCIAL SECURITY...

©1984 M.A.S.

THEN, *Suddenly,* IT CURVED.

...FOR tHE RICH.

BUT THE BATTER CLOBBERED IT *anyway.*

CRRACK!

TAKE **THAT**, YOU **UNFAIR** ELITIST!

House of Reps 1

THAT'S NOT FAIR!

Said the TREASURY SECRETARY.

FAIRNESS, *of course,* WAS VERY MUCH OF CONCERN TO HIM THIS WEEK: "NATIONAL NEUTRALIZE-THE-'FAIRNESS-ISSUE' WEEK."

IT WAS A SPECIAL TIME.

ONCE EVERY FOUR YEARS, WE SET ASIDE THIS WEEK TO SAY BAD THINGS ABOUT RICH PEOPLE.

THIS, HOWEVER, WAS NOT WHAT WAS BOTHERING THE CHAIRMAN OF THE GLOMINOID CORPORATION.

MR. OXBOGGLE, WHAT'S WRONG?

I CAN'T TAKE IT.

ON HIS LAP WAS A MAGAZINE. CONGRESSMAN FOREHEAD PICKED IT UP.

THIS NEVER HAPPENED BEFORE.

BIZMUSWIK THE TOP 25 HIGHEST-PAID EXECUTIVES

I CAME *in* 37th. I'M NOT *in* tHE TOP 25. THE OTHER CHAIRMEN WILL LAUGH AT ME. YOU DON'T KNOW WHAT IT'S LIKE.

I'VE SEEN THEM DO IT TO OTHER CHAIRMEN AT THE COUNTRY CLUB. ONE GUY I KNOW WAS THE 34tH HIGHEST PAID. THE GUYS IN THE "TOP 25" MADE FUN OF HIM UNTIL HE WAS DRIVEN HOME CRYING!...

When the Administration blamed Federal Reserve Board policy for a recent rise in interest rates, Don Smith's reaction was typical of most voters.

JACK'S PIZZA
Plain slice.....$.95
With mushrooms...1.30
pepper.........1.70
onion..........2.30
pickle.........3.15
chocolate syrup...4.60
pecans.........8.50
orange slices....9.80
fruit pizza....15.50
candy pizza....75.09
...UPE...518.40
...1,379.20

I'VE GOT TO CHECK THAT OUT FOR MYSELF!

©1984 M.A.S.

That night after work, Don went to the library.

DO YOU HAVE ANY BOOKS THAT TRACE THE HISTORICAL RELATIONSHIP BETWEEN interest RATES and TARGET LEVELS OF MONETARY AGGREGRATES?

CERTAINLY. THEY'RE VERY POPULAR! EVERYONE WAS TALKING ABOUT IT.

LIBRARIAN

LAST MONTH IT WAS MICHAEL JACKSON. THIS MONTH IT WAS MONETARY POLICY THAT WAS CAPTURING THE IMAGINATION OF AMERICA.

M-1 IS MY FAVORITE AGGREGATE! I JUST WISH THEY'D LOOSEN UP ON IT!

ME TOO! THAT FED IS SO UPTIGHT!

EVEN CHILDREN WERE CATCHING ON.

LET'S PLAY "DUNGEONS AND DRAGONS."

NO! NOT THAT! I WANNA PLAY "FEDERAL RESERVE BOARD"!

OH BOY! YEH! AND I'LL BE THE CHAIRMAN!

NO! IT'S MY TURN!

NO! IT'S MY TURN!

Meanwhile, at a certain exclusive country club, it was Glominoid Chairman Gerard Oxboggle's turn... to tee off.

HEY, GERRY, IF YOU NEED TO BORROW A FEW BUCKS, JUST LET ME KNOW.

SAID ONE OF THE "TOP 25" HIGHEST-PAID EXECUTIVES.

SEVERAL OTHERS FROM THE "TOP 25" LAUGHED.

AS THEY LAUGHED, GERARD, THE 37th HIGHEST-PAID EXECUTIVE, FUMED,

...AND TRIED TO CONJURE AN APPROPRIATE RESPONSE.

FINALLY IT CAME TO HIM.

I KNOW WHAT I'LL DO... I'LL BUY HIM OUT! I'LL BUY THEM ALL OUT! ONE BY ONE...

RECENTLY, THE ADMINISTRATION BEGAN CONDUCTING EXPERIMENTS IN VIDEO-HYPNOSIS.

THIS IS AMERICA.

...THIS IS AMERICA.

...THIS IS **NOT** AMERICA.

...THERE IS NO HUNGER IN AMERICA.

...AMERICA WAS NEVER INVOLVED IN LEBANON.

...THE FEDERAL DEFICIT IS NO CAUSE FOR WORRY.

...AND, BEST OF ALL, WE HAVE A PRESIDENT WHO NEVER COMPLAINS THAT HIS JOB IS TOO HARD...

HERE IS YOUR NEXT SPEECH, MR. PRESIDENT. YOU HAVE ONLY 2 HOURS TO MEMORIZE IT.

NO PROBLEM!

Meanwhile, CONGRESSMAN FOREHEAD WAS CONSIDERING AN EXPERIMENT IN REVENUE-RAISING.

WE COULD DISSOLVE THE TAX SYSTEM ALTOGETHER...

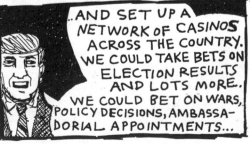

...AND SET UP A NETWORK OF CASINOS ACROSS THE COUNTRY. WE COULD TAKE BETS ON ELECTION RESULTS AND LOTS MORE. WE COULD BET ON WARS, POLICY DECISIONS, AMBASSA-DORIAL APPOINTMENTS...

ONE DAY the PRESIDENT ADDRESSED A GATHERING OF HIS SUPPORTERS.

FOR TOO LONG PARTISAN POLITICS HAS OPERATED BY A SYSTEM OF **M**UTUALLY **A**SSERTED **D**EROGATION IN WHICH EACH SIDE TRIES TO **TOTALLY DESTROY** THE OTHER SIDE IN THE MINDS OF THE VOTERS.

TO CONTINUE IN THIS WAY IS MADNESS!

©1985 M.A.B.

WOULDN'T IT BE BETTER IF THERE WERE A WAY TO CREATE A FORCE FIELD AROUND THE VOTERS' MINDS THAT WOULD LOCK IN A PLEASURABLE PERCEPTION OF **OUR SIDE** AND DIMINISH, AND EVEN ELIMINATE, ANY DESIRE BY THE VOTERS TO THINK THROUGH ISSUES IN ANY DEGREE OF DETAIL?

I BELIEVE THAT SUCH A CAPABILITY IS WITHIN OUR REACH!

SO DID RESEARCHERS AT THE MARYLAND INSTITUTE OF PERCEPTRONICS.

WE'RE ON THE VERGE!

FOR MANY YEARS NOW THEY HAD BEEN TRYING TO DETECT A SUBATOMIC PARTICLE KNOWN AS THE "FUZON."

WHY IS IT SO IMPORTANT?

FUZONS ARE THE CAUSE OF FUZZY-MINDEDNESS. THE ABILITY TO CONTROL THESE FUZONS IS ESSENTIAL TO THE CREATION AND MAINTENANCE OF MANY MASS-INDUCED PERCEPTIONS.

MASS-INDUCED PERCEPTIONS COULD INSPIRE BOB FOREHEAD.

LET YOURSELF FEEL IT! COME ON!...

AND BOB, ON SUCH OCCASIONS, COULD STIR A CROWD TO ECSTATIC DELIRIUM.

FEEL ALL THAT MILITARY **POWER** WE'VE GOT! LET IT SURGE THROUGH YOU! FEEL THOSE MISSILES IN YOUR MUSCLES! FEEL THAT STRONG DOLLAR! NOTHING CAN STOP US!

I DON'T EVEN LIKE TO THINK ABOUT HOW MY LIFE USED TO BE. I HAD A TERRIBLE, LOW-PAYING JOB. I WAS VERY UNHAPPY...

©1984 m.a.s.

...THEN ONE DAY A FRIEND TOLD ME ABOUT A CANDIDATE FOR CONGRESS NAMED BOB FOREHEAD, WHO HAD A NEW VISION OF AMERICA AND WAS ALSO REALLY CUTE.

I VOTED FOR HIM AND HE WON..

...AND TWO MONTHS AFTER HE TOOK OFFICE I GOT A GREAT NEW JOB AT TWICE THE PAY AND MET MY FUTURE HUSBAND. NOW I'M REALLY HAPPY!...

HIS TV ADS WERE EFFECTIVE...

BUT THE CHALLENGER WAS ABLE TO MAKE A DENT.

...BOB FOREHEAD TALKS ABOUT CUTTING MORE TAXES, BUT HE HAS NO SOLUTION FOR THE DEFICIT THAT WILL UNDERMINE THE RECOVERY.

THAT'S NOT TRUE!

SAID BOB.

THE DEFICIT COULD BE ELIMINATED QUICKLY IF THE LIBERALS IN CONGRESS HAD THE GUTS...

...TO SUPPORT MY DEFICIT-DENIAL AMENDMENT, WHICH WOULD LEGALLY DENY THE VERY EXISTENCE OF A FEDERAL DEFICIT. OUR CONSTITUTION IS A POWERFUL TOOL IF WE HAVE THE COURAGE TO USE IT!

IN THE LAST WEEK OF THE CAMPAIGN BOB'S STAFF HIRED SEVERAL SQUADS OF MERCENARY GUERILLA CHIT-CHATTERS, DEPLOYING THEM IN BARS, SUPERMARKETS, DRUGSTORES, BANK LINES. THEIR MISSION: TO BE OVERHEARD.

WITH CASUAL PRECISION, THESE COLD-BLOODED PROFESSIONALS SPREAD THEIR DEADLY PERCEPTION.

WHAT D'YA THINK OF THAT GUY RUNNING AGAINST BOB FOREHEAD?

HE'S A WIMP!

I'LL SAY!

AND THE VOTERS SAID:

WE WANT BOB! WE WANT BOB!

TWO MORE YEARS! TWO MORE YEARS!

AND THE MAGIC STARTED ALL OVER AGAIN.

I'LL ANSWER ANY QUESTIONS.

SAID CONGRESSMAN BOB FOREHEAD.

BOB, **STOP** IT!

Yes, THE LADY IN THE PINK BATHROBE...

©1984 m. a. s.

I SAID **STOP** IT! I'M YOUR **WIFE**! THIS IS **BREAKFAST**! YOU'RE ACTING **CRAZY**!...

WELL, YES, IF I UNDERSTAND YOUR QUESTION CORRECTLY, YOU'RE REFERRING TO MY OPPOSITION TO FEDERALLY-FUNDED BREAKFAST PROGRAMS...

BOB, IT'S **ME**! YOUR **WIFE**! GINGER! THERE'S NOBODY ELSE HERE!

SHE SHOULDN'T HAVE SAID THAT.

WHERE AM I? **WHO** AM I?... EVERYTHING IS DARK! ...I FEEL SO ALONE!...

BOB, I'M **HERE**! I'M YOUR **WIFE**!...

THE DOCTOR WAS ABLE TO EXPLAIN.

CAMPAIGNINGITIS.

HE MUST HAVE ENDED HIS CAMPAIGN TOO ABRUPTLY. IT'S DANGEROUS FOR HIM NOW TO BE IN A ROOM WITH FEWER THAN FIFTY PEOPLE HANGING ON HIS EVERY WORD...

BUT, DOCTOR, WE CAN'T HAVE FIFTY PEOPLE LIVING IN OUR HOUSE!

THE OTHER POSSIBILITY IS THESE CORRECTIVE GLASSES. IN A WEEK OR TWO, HE SHOULD BE ALL RIGHT.

THE DOCTOR FITTED THE GLASSES ON BOB. BOB LOOKED AT GINGER AND SAW:

NOW **CHEER** HIM! APPLAUD HIM! SHOUT **HIS** NAME!

WE WANT BOB! WE WANT BOB!

NO ONE HAD EVER TOLD GINGER THAT MARRIAGE WAS EASY.

YA-A-AY, BOB!!

SWAMI POLLSTERNANDA

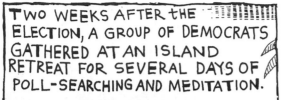

TWO WEEKS AFTER THE ELECTION, A GROUP OF DEMOCRATS GATHERED AT AN ISLAND RETREAT FOR SEVERAL DAYS OF POLL-SEARCHING AND MEDITATION.

RELAX...

CLEAR YOUR MIND OF ALL DISTRACTIONS AND FOCUS ON THE CENTER.

SAID SWAMI POLLSTERNANDA.

©1984 M.O.S.

I REALIZE IT WILL BE DIFFICULT FOR MANY OF YOU. YOU'LL FIND THAT YOUR MIND IS CLUTTERED WITH THOUGHTS, IMAGES, AND POSITION PAPERS OF VARIOUS INTEREST GROUPS.

DO NOT LET THEM DISTRACT YOU.

WHENEVER THESE THOUGHTS OCCUR, JUST MEDITATE ON THE RESULTS OF THE THE ELECTORAL VOTE, AND THE DISTRACTIONS WILL LOSE THEIR IMPORTANCE.

SOON THEY WILL HAVE NO POWER OVER YOU,

AND YOU WILL BEGIN TO GET IN TOUCH WITH THE PUBLIC OPINION POLL INSIDE YOU. SURRENDER TO IT. LET IT BE YOUR GUIDE.

ONE CONGRESSMAN, WHO HAD NARROWLY WON RE-ELECTION, HAD A POWERFUL EXPERIENCE DURING THE MEDITATION.

I...I FEEL MY LIBERALISM LIFTING OUT OF ME... I...I'M BEING PULLED TO THE RIGHT... I...I'M ATTRACTING PAC MONEY! AND THE YUPPIE VOTE!

meanwhile, ELSEWHERE, A CONGRESSMAN FROM THE OTHER PARTY WAS ATTRACTING A LOT OF attention.

HELP! HELP! THE MODERATES ARE COMING! THE MODERATES ARE COMING!

THE PESTICIDE RESIDUE COMMITTEE

THAT FIRST WEEK in WASHINGTON WAS very INTENSE FOR CONGRESSMAN-ELECT FLEAGLEY.

I'M GONNA TURN THIS PLACE AROUND!

HE HAD A LOT ON HIS MIND.

HE WAS VERY CONCERNED ABOUT HIS PLACE IN HISTORY.

GENERAL WILLIAM CRAMNOODLE

CONGRESSMAN JEROME FLEAGLEY

A LOT OF THE BEST SPOTS ARE ALREADY TAKEN!

© 1984 m.a.s.

I'D BETTER WORK **FAST!**

OF CRITICAL IMPORTANCE WAS GETTING APPOINTED TO A POWERFUL COMMITTEE.

HOW ABOUT FOREIGN RELATIONS? ...OR BANKING? ...OR BUDGET?

HE DIDN'T GET EXACTLY WHAT HE WANTED.

THE "PESTICIDE RESIDUE COMMITTEE"?!!

WE **NEED** YOU THERE, JERRY!

...JUST AS GINGER FOREHEAD NEEDED HER HUSBAND, BOB, TO EXPLAIN CERTAIN THINGS ABOUT POLITICS THAT PUZZLED HER.

I DON'T GET IT...

...BY THE TIME WE EVER GET STAR WARS, THE PRESIDENT WILL BE LONG OUT OF OFFICE. SO HOW COULD HE EVER POSSIBLY "SHARE" IT WITH RUSSIA?

...AND WHY DID HE SAY HE WOULD?

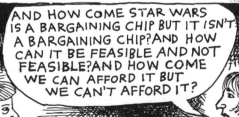

AND HOW COME STAR WARS IS A BARGAINING CHIP BUT IT ISN'T A BARGAINING CHIP? AND HOW CAN IT BE FEASIBLE AND NOT FEASIBLE? AND HOW COME WE CAN AFFORD IT BUT WE CAN'T AFFORD IT?

AND WHO DECIDES WHO IS AN "EXPERT"?!

BOB, AS ALWAYS, HAD THE ANSWER.

BECAUSE, GINGER. **BECAUSE!**

OH.

IF YOU SAW HIM IN A STORE SOMEWHERE, OR ON THE STREET, YOU might NOT take MUCH NOTICE.

HE WASN'T PARTICULARLY charismatic.

©1985 M.A.B.

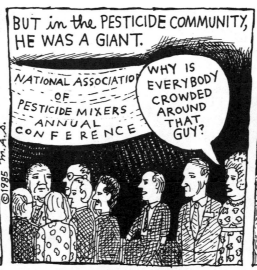

BUT in the PESTICIDE COMMUNITY, HE WAS A GIANT.

NATIONAL ASSOCIATION OF PESTICIDE MIXERS ANNUAL CONFERENCE

WHY IS EVERYBODY CROWDED AROUND THAT GUY?

THE REASON WAS SIMPLE:

FEFPIFA.

WHAT?

THE "FEDERAL ENVIRONMENTAL FRAGRANCE OF PESTICIDES INSPECTION FREQUENCY ACT."
HE WROTE IT.

"HE" WAS CONGRESSMAN JIM BOIZLE, and "FEFPIFA" WAS LIKE A DAUGHTER TO HIM.

ALSO PRESENT WAS FRESHMAN CONGRESSMAN JERRY FLEAGLEY.

THE PESTICIDE INDUSTRY IS BEING CRIPPLED BY A TERRIBLE BLIGHT. THE NAME OF THAT BLIGHT IS "FEFPIFA"!

WITH THIS BOLD ASSAULT ON A VETERAN COLLEAGUE, JERRY FLEAGLEY MANAGED TO FUEL SPECULATION AMONG TWO PUNDITS in THE BACK OF THE ROOM.

HE'S TAPPING A RESERVOIR OF RESENTMENT. "FEFPIFA" COULD BE IN TROUBLE!

THIS GUY LOOKS LIKE an UP-AND-COMER!

HE SURE DOES! AND HE'S GOT A SENATE SEAT OPENING UP IN '88.

I SAY HE'LL MAKE A RUN FOR THE WHITE HOUSE IN '92.

IF HE WINS, DO YOU THINK HE'LL GO FOR A SECOND TERM?

I'D SAY THAT WOULD DEPEND ON THE ECONOMY.

SEATED NEARBY WAS CONGRESSMAN BOB FOREHEAD.

THAT WAS MORE SPECULATION THAN I FUELED IN MY ENTIRE PRESIDENTIAL CAMPAIGN!

GIVE IT TIME, BOB. GIVE IT TIME.

GENEVA, SWITZERLAND. 2:15 P.M. THE U.S. ARMS CONTROL NEGOTIATORS HAD JUST RETURNED FROM LUNCH and WERE WAITING FOR their SOVIET COUNTERPARTS.

WHERE ARE THEY?

THEY MUST BE LATE.

©1985 m.a.s.

BY 3:05, HOWEVER, THE U.S. DELEGATION BEGAN TO SENSE TROUBLE.

THEY CAN'T BE **THIS** LATE! THEY MUST HAVE WALKED OUT ON THE TALKS.

QUICK! CALL WASHINGTON!

THEY RAN TO THE PHONE.

HELLO, MR. PRESIDENT. THE SOVIETS HAVE WALKED OUT ON THE ARMS TALKS! WE NEED YOUR HELP TO GET THEM BACK!...

I'LL GET RIGHT ON IT!

IMMEDIATELY the PRESIDENT WENT ON TELEVISION, ADDRESSING CONGRESS and THE AMERICAN PEOPLE.

...THE ONLY WAY TO GET the SOVIETS BACK to the TABLE IS FOR CONGRESS to APPROVE MY NEW PACKAGE OF 80 BILLION DOLLARS iN ADDITIONAL NUCLEAR WEAPONS!...

ANXIOUS FOR AN END TO the ARMS RACE, the AMERICAN PEOPLE DELUGED their LAWMAKERS WITH PHONE CALLS SUPPORTING the PRESIDENT.

THE BILL SPED THROUGH CONGRESS.

80 BILLION DOLLARS IS A **SMALL PRICE** TO PAY FOR A CHANCE TO MAKE AN AGREEMENT TO DISMANTLE THESE NEW WEAPONS AS SOON AS WE FINISH BUILDING THEM!

AT 4:49 P.M. GENEVA TIME, THE BILL BECAME LAW.

FIVE MINUTES LATER THE SOVIET DELEGATION CAME RUSHING IN.

SORRY WE'RE LATE. WE DID SOME SHOPPING AFTER LUNCH AND LOST TRACK OF THE TIME. THEN WE GOT CAUGHT IN TRAFFIC...

THAT NIGHT THE U.S. DELEGATION CELEBRATED THEIR VICTORY.

DID YOU SEE HOW FAST THEY GAVE IN?!

WE'VE GOT THEM IN THE PALMS OF OUR HANDS!

ONCE AN ELUSIVE DREAM, ARMS CONTROL SEEMED SUDDENLY WITHIN THEIR GRASP.

WHOOPEE!

LET'S RUN THROUGH IT AGAIN.

©1985 M.A.S.

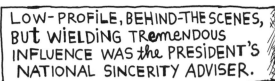

LOW-PROFILE, BEHIND-THE-SCENES, BUT WIELDING TREMENDOUS INFLUENCE WAS the PRESIDENT'S NATIONAL SINCERITY ADVISER.

...AS LONG AS THEY BELIEVE THAT YOU BELIEVE, the FUZONS WILL BE ACTIVATED.

SOMETIMES HIS JOB REQUIRED HIM TO ADVISE THE PRESIDENT ON CHANGES IN POLICY.

I THINK MAYBE WE SHOULD CUT BACK ON THE AMOUNT OF PROBLEMS THAT WE BLAME ON PAST ADMINISTRATIONS.

ADDRESSING A TEST GROUP OF SELECTED VOTERS, THEY TRIED OUT A NEW APPROACH.

THE RECENT SLOWDOWN IN ECONOMIC GROWTH IS A DIRECT RESULT OF A LACK OF CONFIDENCE IN THE **FAILED POLICIES** OF FUTURE ADMINISTRATIONS.

THE NATIONAL SINCERITY ADVISER OBSERVED QUIETLY AS FUZONIC RAPTURE ENSCONCED THE FACES IN THE CROWD.

FFZZZZZZ   FFZZZZZZ   FFZZZZZZ

MEANWHILE, ANOTHER FORM OF RAPTURE WAS BEING WITNESSED BY CONGRESSMAN FOREHEAD.

IT'S GOING TO BE BIG! VERY BIG! WE'VE TESTED IT!

THE KILTEK CORPORATION HAD DEVELOPED A NEW BREAKFAST CEREAL.

Kiltek
SUGAR DEFENSE INITIATIVE CRISPIES

BOB OPENED THE BOX AND THE CRISPIES WENT INTO ORBIT AROUND THE BOWL.

HOW DO YOU EAT THEM?

LIKE THIS!

FLIM

GOOD EVENING. I'M BOB FOREHEAD WITH THE NEWS. OUR TOP STORY: CONGRESSMAN BOB FOREHEAD TODAY CALLED FOR A TOUGHER STANCE TOWARD THE SOVIET UNION.

AFTERWARDS, I SPOKE WITH MYSELF IN THIS **EXCLUSIVE INTERVIEW**:

CONGRESSMAN, *in your opinion,* WHAT IS THE GREATEST THREAT TO OUR NATIONAL SECURITY?... BOB, I HAVE DOCUMENTED **PROOF** THAT NUMEROUS PERSONS IN **KEY** POSITIONS IN OUR FEDERAL GOVERNMENT ARE **KNOWN WIMPS!**

WAS IT JUST A DREAM? COULD IT REALLY COME TRUE?

MY OWN TV SHOW?!

IT'S POSSIBLE...

...IF YOU GET IN WITH US EARLY.

SAID THE SENATOR, WHO BELONGED TO A GROUP CALLED "**FLIM**," ("FIRE LIBERALS IN MEDIA").

©1985 M.A.S.

THAT NIGHT BOB GAVE A SPEECH.

THERE IS A TERRIBLE BLIGHT *THAT IS* DISENHANCING OUR EXERCISE OF FREEDOM IN AMERICA.

I UNDERSTAND NOW THAT WE WILL NEVER BE TRULY FREE UNTIL WE...

...GET GOVERNMENT **OUT OF** GOVERNMENT!

THE FUTURE OF DEMOCRACY RESTS ON TWO GREAT PILLARS: MONEY AND TELEVISION. WE MUST CHERISH THESE TOOLS AND NURTURE THEM...

Meanwhile, NEARBY SAT BOB'S CHERISHED WIFE GINGER, NURTURING A DISTURBING THOUGHT:

AM I REALLY MARRIED TO THIS GUY?

..FLIP-FLOP, FLIP-FLOP, FLIP-FLOP, FLIP-FLOP,...

IT WAS A GIFT TO CONGRESSMAN FOREHEAD FROM HIS STAFF.

©1985 m.a.s.

GEE, THANKS. ...IT FITS JUST RIGHT. ...WHAT **IS** IT?

A SWITCH WATCH.

...FLIP-FLOP, FLIP-FLOP, FLIP-FLOP, FLIP-FLOP,...

IT'S THE NEWEST THING! LOTS OF POLITICIANS ARE GETTING THEM.

HOW DO YOU READ IT? IT HAS SO MANY HANDS.

YES, *and* EACH HAND IS A DIFFERENT ISSUE,...

...AND THE NUMBERS REPRESENT MONTHS,...

...AND EVERY TIME YOU TAKE A STRONG POSITION ON AN ISSUE YOU SET THAT HAND AT ZERO. BY **4 O'CLOCK V.A.T.**, OR "**VOTER AMNESIA TIME**", THE VOTERS WILL NO LONGER REMEMBER WHAT YOU SAID, AND YOU CAN SAFELY REVERSE YOUR POSITION!

BOB GOT SO EXCITED ABOUT HIS *new* WATCH THAT HE LOST TRACK OF THE *time*.

I'M LATE!

HE CAUGHT THE LAST HALF OF THE SEMINAR.

THIS IS A MODEL OF THE ICBC-MM BETTER KNOWN AS THE MOOD MISSILE.

THIS STATE OF THE ART *Intercontinental* BARGAINING **CHIP** HAS A LAUNCHING DEVICE *that can* BE TRIGGERED BY RESULTS OF A PUBLIC OPINION POLL.

AS SOON AS 51% OF AMERICANS THINK AMERICA IS "WEAK", THIS MISSILE WILL AUTOMAT-ICALLY FIRE!

BOB WAS FIRED UP TOO, REVELLING IN THE GLORIES OF MODERN TECHNOLOGY.

AMERICA WAS TRIMMING DOWN.

...LET'S GO, AMERICA! **SHAKE-OUT** ALL THOSE EXCESS FARMERS! ...DOESN'T IT FEEL **GOOD**?!!

©1985 m.A.8.

NOT TO GINGER FOREHEAD IT DIDN'T.

IT DOESN'T SEEM RIGHT! I mean, THEY GOT SOME BAD ADVICE, THEY HAD A BAD BREAK...

GINGER, GET **WITH** IT! THAT WAS **LAST** MONTH'S ISSUE! IT'S OVER! IT'S OFF THE CHARTS!

I CAN'T KEEP UP WITH ALL THESE ISSUES THE WAY YOU DO...

DID YOU GET MAD AT JAPAN YET?

NO.

WELL, HURRY UP! YOU'RE WAY BEHIND!

I'M STILL MAD ABOUT FISH. IT SEEMS LIKE EVERY DAY THEY TELL YOU ANOTHER KIND OF FISH THAT'S TOO CONTAMINATED TO EAT!

THAT'S CHANGE, GINGER! ...**PROGRESS**!

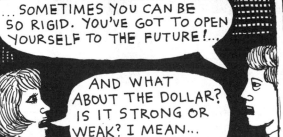

...SOMETIMES YOU CAN BE SO RIGID. YOU'VE GOT TO OPEN YOURSELF TO THE FUTURE!...

AND WHAT ABOUT THE DOLLAR? IS IT STRONG OR WEAK? I MEAN...

...IF THE DOLLAR IS SO "STRONG", HOW COME IT'S **WEAKENING** US? I MEAN, WHOSE DOLLAR **IS** IT ANYWAY?...

IF WE CAN'T STOP IT FROM HURTING US, AND AND ECONOMISTS DON'T EVEN KNOW WHY IT'S SO "STRONG" OR WHEN IT'S GOING TO WEAKEN...

IS THE DOLLAR **ALIVE**? DOES IT HAVE A BRAIN? DOES IT HAVE A WILL OF ITS OWN?...

CONGRESSMAN FOREHEAD SAID NOTHING. HE STARED AT HIS WIFE. IT WAS HAPPENING AGAIN. THEY WEREN'T COMMUNICATING. LIKE TWO SEPARATE PLANETS. HOW LONG COULD THEY GO ON THIS WAY?

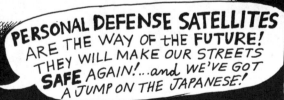

WELCOME TO "NEWSNOISE," WITH ALL THE NEWS ABOUT THE NEWS, BEHIND THE NEWS, AND EVERY SIDE OF THE NEWS. TONIGHT'S TOPIC:

NEWS. WHAT **IS** NEWS? WHAT **ISN'T** NEWS?

FOR ONE OPINION, WE TURN TO VETERAN CORRESPONDENT JOHN JABBER.

...JOHN, IF SOMETHING **ISN'T** NEWS BUT GETS REPORTED **AS** NEWS, DOES IT THEN **BECOME** NEWS, OR DOES IT REMAIN **NON**-NEWS THAT MANY PEOPLE MISTAKENLY BELIEVE TO **BE** NEWS AND IS THAT BELIEF THAT THE NON-NEWS IS NEWS **NEWS**? ...

© 1985 M.A.B.

WELL, FIRST OF ALL, I THINK WE MUST EXAMINE WHAT WE MEAN WHEN WE USE THE TERM "NEWS"...

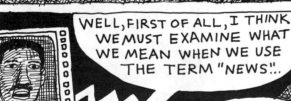

BILL, I HAVE A FEELING...

SHH. IT'S JUST GETTING TO THE GOOD PART.

BILL, TALK TO ME!

SAID THE WASHINGTON SPOUSE, RECOGNIZING THE EARLY SIGNS.

OH NO!

HE WAS ON A NEWS BINGE.

BILL, FIGHT IT! RESIST IT!...

YOU'RE IN MY WAY...

THE LAST ONE HAD GONE ON FOR THREE WEEKS. IT WAS TWO MORE DAYS BEFORE HE RECOGNIZED HER.

DON'T DO IT, BILL! DON'T DO IT!

I HAVE TO. I HAVE TO.

WAIT FOR ME.

I DON'T KNOW IF I **CAN** THIS TIME.

AND NOW FOR MORE NEWS...

CLEARLY, THE NICARAGUAN GOVERNMENT PRESENTS AN IMMINENT DANGER TO OUR NATIONAL SECURITY...

SAID THE FOREIGN POLICY EXPERT.

I CAN HARDLY BELIEVE THAT A TINY NATION OF THREE MILLION PEOPLE COULD POSE SUCH A THREAT...

SAID THE OTHER FOREIGN POLICY EXPERT.

...THE NICARAGUAN PEOPLE WILL RISE UP AGAINST THEIR GOVERNMENT AS SOON AS WE GIVE THEM OUR SUPPORT...

NO. THEY'D RISE UP AGAINST US!

© 1985 M.A.S.

THIS IS THE MOST URGENT CRISIS FACING OUR NATION TODAY!

WE HAVE NO BUSINESS MEDDLING IN THE INTERNAL AFFAIRS OF A SOVEREIGN NATION...

IF WE DON'T SUPPORT THE "FREEDOM FIGHTERS" NOW, WE WILL HAVE COMMUNISTS IN OUR BACKYARDS.

NICARAGUA IS A TINY, TINY...

THEIR ARMY IS GETTING BIGGER AND BIGGER!...

I'M BEGINNING TO GET THE HANG OF THIS...

NICARAGUA CAN BE **ANYTHING** WE WANT IT TO BE! EACH OF US CAN IMAGINE IT HOWEVER WE WANT.

MOST OF US WILL NEVER VISIT NICARAGUA, SO, IN CASE WE MAKE A MESS OF THINGS DOWN THERE, ALL WE HAVE TO DO IS NOT WATCH THE NEWS FOR A FEW WEEKS.

I WONDER WHAT DEMOCRACY WAS LIKE BEFORE THEY DEVELOPED REMOTE CONTROL.

FLICK

LINKAGE

IN YOUR OPINION, HAVE WE OVERDONE OUR COVERAGE OF OUR COVERAGE OF OUR COVERAGE OF THE HOSTAGE CRISIS?

WELL, THAT IS A VERY COMPLICATED QUESTION, WHICH I HOPE TO PUT INTO CLEARER PERSPECTIVE WITH AN UPCOMING EIGHT-PART DOCUMENTARY...

©1985 M.A.&

PUTTING COMPLICATED QUESTIONS INTO CLEARER PERSPECTIVE WAS NOTHING NEW TO CONGRESSMAN BOB FOREHEAD.

TAX REFORM MEANS A TAX CUT FOR **YOU**.

THAT SOUNDS FAIR!

DEFENSE SPENDING MEANS **JOBS**!

ALL THIRD WORLD CONFLICTS ARE SIMPLY SOVIET THREATS TO OUR FREEDOM!

BUT SOME OF BOB'S POLITICAL VIEWS POSED THREATS TO HIS MARRIAGE.

YOU'RE SO SIMPLISTIC!

SAID HIS WIFE, GINGER.

THE WORLD IS MORE COMPLICATED THAN THAT! YOU SUPPORT FOREIGN POLICIES ABOUT PEOPLE YOU DON'T EVEN UNDERSTAND!

TO QUIET GINGER DOWN, BOB DECIDED TO GO ON A FACT-FINDING MISSION.

SEE YOU NEXT WEEK.

AMONG THE FACTS HE FOUND WERE: WHICH HOTEL HAD THE BEST TENNIS COURTS AND WHICH BAR HAD THE BEST PIÑA COLADAS.

IT WAS A VERY SUCCESSFUL TRIP.

FORGET ABOUT REDUCING THE DEFICIT! THAT'S BESIDE THE POINT!

WHAT IS THE POINT?

REDUCING THE DEFICIT REQUIRES CERTAIN PEOPLE TO TAKE THE BLAME FOR CERTAIN OTHER PEOPLE'S HARDSHIPS. IT GETS TOO SPECIFIC. AND POLITICALLY HARMFUL.

© 1985 m.a.l.

THE WHOLE POINT IS TO DIFFUSE THE BLAME SO THAT EVERYBODY HAS SOMEONE TO BLAME. ...EVEN THE PEOPLE WHO ARE TO BLAME.

...AND EVERYBODY GETS TO URGE SOME TYPE OF BUDGET CUTS, NONE OF WHICH CAN ATTRACT ENOUGH SUPPORT TO PASS. SO EVERYONE CAN FEEL INNOCENT.

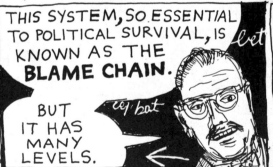

THIS SYSTEM, SO ESSENTIAL TO POLITICAL SURVIVAL, IS KNOWN AS THE BLAME CHAIN.

BUT IT HAS MANY LEVELS.

A GIFTED FEW BECOME BLAME MASTERS. THEIR SECRET IS AN UNDERSTANDING OF BLAME ENERGY IN ITS PUREST FORM.

TO THESE MASTERS, ISSUES ARE IRRELEVANT. IN ANY SITUATION, THEY CAN CONTROL BLAME ENERGY...

AND DIRECT ITS AWESOME POWER AT ANY OPPONENT WITH DEVASTATING FORCE, LEAVING THEIR VICTIM DEFEATED AND MYSTIFIED.

THE POLITICIANS IN THE CLASSROOM GAZED SHYLY AROUND AT ONE ANOTHER, A DREAM GLOWING IN THEIR EYES.

COME ON, AMERICA! EAT UP!

TAX TRIM TREATS

ANTI COMMIE YUMMIES

BUDGET BALONEY

U.S.A.

© 1985 M.A.S.

NO ONE HAD TO SAY THAT TO CONGRESSMAN BOB FOREHEAD AT AN OUTDOOR FAIR IN HIS HOME DISTRICT.

HE WAS MAKING AN EFFORT TO EAT, CHAT, KID AROUND AND ELICIT A CERTAIN REACTION AMONG THOSE PRESENT.

LOOK AT HOW **HUMAN** HE IS!

HE ACTS JUST LIKE A **REGULAR** PERSON!

HE WAS BEGINNING TO ENJOY HIMSELF WHEN, SUDDENLY, ONE OF THE VOTERS GOT SUBSTANTIVE.

WHAT WAS YOUR POSITION ON OIL IMPORT FEES?

I OPPOSED THEM.

WHY?

BECAUSE THE LAST ELECTION PROVED THAT AMERICANS OPPOSE ANY AND ALL NEW TAXES.

I DON'T BELIEVE THAT. SOME NEW TAXES WOULD HELP CUT THE DEFICIT.

THE LAST ELECTION PROVED THAT AMERICANS BELIEVE THAT PEOPLE WHO WORRY ABOUT THE DEFICIT ARE WEAK, NEGATIVE WIMPS!

BUT ALL OF THAT HAS **CHANGED!** NOW PEOPLE **ARE** WORRIED ABOUT IT! THEY WANT SOMETHING TO BE DONE!

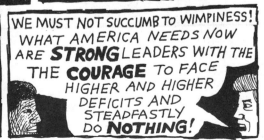

WE MUST NOT SUCCUMB TO WIMPINESS! WHAT AMERICA NEEDS NOW ARE **STRONG** LEADERS WITH THE THE **COURAGE** TO FACE HIGHER AND HIGHER DEFICITS AND STEADFASTLY DO **NOTHING!**

THE WASHINGTON MONUMENT WAS STILL POPULAR, ...AND THE CAPITOL DOME, AND THE LINCOLN MEMORIAL, ALL VERY IMPRESSIVE.

BUT, LATELY, ANOTHER WASHINGTON STRUCTURE WAS ATTRACTING EVER LARGER NUMBERS OF TOURISTS.

AMAZING!

AWESOME!

BREATH-TAKING!

HOLD IT! LET ME GET ANOTHER PICTURE. SMILE!

©1985 m.a.s.

A SPECIAL ELEVATOR ALLOWED VISITORS AN AERIAL VIEW OF THE FAMOUS STRUCTURE WHILE TOURGUIDES EXPLAINED:

...THIS IS OUR NATIONAL DEBT, THE LARGEST PILE OF PHOTOCOPIED I.O.U.'S IN THE ENTIRE WORLD!

GUIDE

GOSH!

WOW!

THAT'S AMERICA FOR YA?! ALWAYS THE BEST!

UNLIKE AMERICA, CONGRESSMAN FOREHEAD WAS SOMETIMES LESS THAN BEST, ... ESPECIALLY AT THE END OF A LONG WEEK.

ONE MORE SPEECH TO GO, BOB!

OH, BROTHER! I'M EXHAUSTED! ...SO WHO'S NEXT?

"THE ASSOCIATION FOR DISASSOCIATION." THERE ARE THOUSANDS OF CHAPTERS ACROSS THE NATION...

EACH CHAPTER HAS ONLY ONE MEMBER. THEY BELIEVE THAT IF PEOPLE WOULD STOP ASSOCIATING WITH ONE ANOTHER, THERE WOULD BE NO WARS.

BOB ENTERED THE AUDITORIUM. THERE WAS ONE PERSON IN THE AUDIENCE. AS SOON AS BOB BEGAN HIS SPEECH, THE PERSON STOOD UP AND WALKED OUT.

GOOD JOB, BOB! I SCHEDULED THIS GROUP LAST BECAUSE I KNEW YOU'D BE TIRED.

GOOD THINKING! THAT WORKED OUT JUST RIGHT!

LOOK ME STRAIGHT IN THE EYE, BOB, AND TELL ME YOU BELIEVE IT.

YOU REALLY LIKE TO ANALYZE THINGS TO DEATH, DON'T YOU, GINGER?

SAID CONGRESSMAN FOREHEAD.

© 1985 M.A.B.

JUST TELL ME, PLEASE, HOW A "BALANCED BUDGET AMENDMENT" IS GOING TO SUDDENLY MAKE THE BUDGET BE BALANCED!

HOW ABOUT IF WE HAVE AN ISSUE-FREE VACATION?

OH, ALL RIGHT.

YOUR CHOICE OF SOFTWARE IS UNDOUBTEDLY THE MOST IMPORTANT DECISION OF YOUR CAMPAIGN,

©1985 M.A.S.

...MORE IMPORTANT THAN EVEN YOUR CHOICE OF A CANDIDATE, AND THIS HAS BEEN PROVEN. LAST YEAR "ELECT-EZE" SELECTED FIVE PERSONS AND RAN THEM FOR HIGH POLITICAL OFFICES...

...FOR WHICH THEY WERE ALL TOTALLY UNQUALIFIED.

NOW, THAT IS THE REAL TEST.

AND WE ARE PLEASED TO SAY THAT ALL FIVE ARE NOW SERVING IN THOSE OFFICES.

THAT'S VERY IMPRESSIVE. HOW DOES IT WORK?

WELL, FIRST OF ALL, BY DEBUNKING THE MYTH THAT VOTERS ARE INDIVIDUALS WITH MINDS OF THEIR OWN. **AXIOM NUMBER ONE:** THERE IS NO SUCH THING AS A PERSONAL THOUGHT. PEOPLE THINK IN HUGE "BLOCKS" SIMULTANEOUSLY.

ANY TIME ANY PERSON THINKS ANY SORT OF THOUGHT, THERE ARE **THOUSANDS** OF OTHER PEOPLE THINKING IT WITH HIM.

"ELECT-EZE" HAS COMPILED HUNDREDS OF COMPUTER DISKETTES OF VOTER LISTS OF ALL MAJOR AND MINOR THOUGHT BLOCKS.

VOTERS ARE LIKE FISH. WE TEACH YOU HOW TO LAY YOUR NET, THROW OUT THE BAIT, AND HAUL THEM IN.

IT WAS A HEADY SENSATION TO CARRY THE WILL OF A NATION IN A BRIEFCASE.

HE TORE OUT THE ARTICLE FROM THE NEWSPAPER AND CIRCLED THE LAST TWO WORDS OF THE HEADLINE.

IT SERVED AS POIGNANT TESTIMONY TO HIS DEEPLY HELD CONVICTION:

GUNS DON'T KILL PEOPLE. ...PEOPLE KILL GUNS!

N.R.A.

NATIONAL RIOT ASSOCIATION

IT WAS A FRIGHTENING TIME FOR GUN OWNERS.

I LEFT MY GUNS AT HOME ALONE. I HOPE THEY'LL BE SAFE!

ON THE FEDERAL LEVEL, THESE FEARS WERE BEING CLOSELY MONITORED BY STAFFERS AT THE BUREAU OF FEAR MANAGEMENT.

GUN OWNER FEARS UP 7.2%.

GOOD! GOOD! NOW LET'S LEVEL OFF.

IT WAS A DIFFICULT TIME AT B.F.M. THE PRESSURE FROM HIGHER UP WAS INCREDIBLE.

WE'RE NOT SEEING ENOUGH MOVEMENT ON THE T.P.F.'s.

THE T.P.F.'s WERE "TOP PRIORITY FEARS."

LET ME SEE THOSE CHARTS.

HIGH AMONG THE T.P.F.'s WAS: FEAR OF THE NICARAGUAN GOVERNMENT.

IT'S JUST NOT MOVING FAST ENOUGH!

WE NEED PANIC, HYSTERIA, OBSESSION!... OUR JOBS ARE ON THE LINE!

THAT WAS ALL IT TOOK: A FEW ANXIOUS WORDS, A FOCUSING OF TERROR AND THE FEARCRAFTERS' ADRENALINE WAS REPLENISHED.

WE CAN DO IT! WE'VE GOT TO! WE WILL!

INTERNAL REVENUE SERVICE

HE LOOKS READY FOR LEVEL TWO.

I THINK YOU'RE RIGHT.

WHEN HIS NUMBER WAS CALLED, HE SAT DOWN WITH AN I.R.S. OFFICIAL.

I FILED MY TAXES IN JANUARY! I'M SUPPOSED TO GET A REFUND! IT'S BEEN ELEVEN MONTHS AND NOTHING! I KEEP CALLING AND I KEEP...

©1985 M.A.S.

...WRITING LETTERS, AND NO ONE I CALL EVER HAS THE AUTHORITY TO SOLVE MY PROBLEM, AND THEY KEEP REFERRING ME TO OTHER PEOPLE WHO DON'T HAVE THE AUTHORITY, OR ELSE I GET BUSY SIGNALS ...

AND I KEEP GETTING LETTERS FROM COMPUTERS THAT HAVEN'T READ **MY** LETTERS...

YOU WANT YOUR MONEY, DON'T YOU, SIR?

YES. EXACTLY.

THAT'S WHERE YOU'VE GONE WRONG.

WHAT DO YOU MEAN?

YOU'RE PLACING TOO MUCH EMPHASIS ON THE GOAL AND NOT ALLOWING YOURSELF TO ENJOY THE **PROCESS.** ...

MAYBE SO...

NO DOUBT THIS IS SYMPTOMATIC OF YOUR LIFE AS A WHOLE.

HOW DID YOU KNOW?

YOU ARE NOT THE FIRST.

MANY PEOPLE THINK THE TERM "INTERNAL REVENUE" REFERS SOMEHOW TO MONEY, BUT THEY ARE MISTAKEN. THE INTERNAL REVENUE WE SPEAK OF IS THE INTERNAL **SPIRITUAL** REVENUE THAT ACCRUES TO YOU WHEN YOU PARTICIPATE IN OUR PROCESS.

AT PRESENT, YOU ARE TENSE, ANXIOUS, CONSUMED WITH DESIRE FOR YOUR REFUND, AND UNABLE TO ACCEPT REALITY AND LIVE FULLY IN THE PRESENT.

BUT EACH COMPUTERIZED LETTER, EACH FUTILE PHONE CALL WILL BRING YOU CLOSER TO A STATE OF CALM RESIGNATION AND INNER PEACE.

WHEN YOU FINALLY RECEIVE YOUR REFUND, IF YOU EVER DO, IT WON'T MATTER. YOU WILL HAVE FOUND SOMETHING OF MUCH GREATER VALUE.

REALLY?! IS THAT REALLY TRUE?!!

TRUST US.

"YOU'RE SURE ABOUT THIS?"

"BOB, NOT ONLY IS IT GOOD POLITICS..."

"...IT'S GOOD **POLICY**! IT PUTS YOU OUT FRONT ON THE NUMBER ONE ISSUE! YOU IRON OUT A MAJOR KINK AND YOU BECOME A KEY PLAYER! THIS COULD TRANSLATE INTO BIG POINTS NATIONALLY!"

©1985 M.A.S.

THAT AFTERNOON CONGRESSMAN FOREHEAD ADDRESSED HIS COLLEAGUES.

"WE HAVE ACHIEVED A GREAT MILESTONE WITH THE PASSAGE OF A BILL MANDATING ELIMINATION OF THE DEFICIT BY 1991."

"THE FINANCIAL COMMUNITY AND ALL OF THE AMERICAN PEOPLE HAVE BEEN REASSURED BY THIS **TOUGH ACTION**, AND WE CAN BE PROUD!"

"...**BUT ONE GLARING IMPERFECTION REMAINS**...."

"IN 1986 AND *in* EACH ENSUING YEAR UNTIL 1991, WE WILL BE FACED WITH A TERRIBLE FISCAL AND POLITICAL CRISIS, WHICH COULD UPSET THE DELICATE PSYCHOLOGICAL UPLIFT WHICH THE NEW LAW HAS ACHIEVED."

"I, FOR ONE, DO NOT WISH TO SEE US BE PASSIVE VICTIMS OF A CRUEL, IMPERSONAL FUTURE. RATHER, LET US **TAKE ACTION** TO **CONTROL** THAT FUTURE!"

"IN THIS SPIRIT, I INTRODUCE "THE 1985 EXTENSION ACT OF 1985", WHICH WOULD EXTEND THE YEAR 1985 FOR 365 MORE DAYS, AT WHICH TIME..."

"...ON DECEMBER 396th, 1985, WE WILL VOTE ON A POSSIBLE FURTHER EXTENSION."

THE REACTION WAS SLOW, BUT AFTER THEY HAD TIME TO THINK ABOUT IT, SEVERAL OF BOB'S COLLEAGUES CONGRATULATED HIM. HE BEGAN TO SENSE A MOMENTUM. "NICE WORK, BOB!"

...WHAT WE'VE DONE, YOU SEE, IS TAKEN THAT FROM THERE AND PUT THIS OVER HERE SO THAT THE ONES ABOVE THIS CAN COUNTERBALANCE THE ONES OVER UNDER THAT...

MEGAVISION

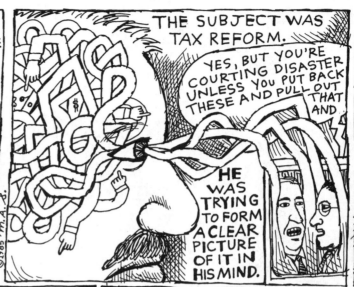

THE SUBJECT WAS TAX REFORM.

YES, BUT YOU'RE COURTING DISASTER UNLESS YOU PUT BACK THESE AND PULL OUT THAT AND

HE WAS TRYING TO FORM A CLEAR PICTURE OF IT IN HIS MIND.

©1985 M.A.S.

THEN THE MODERATOR INTERVENED.

ACCORDING TO POLLS, VOTERS ARE CONFUSED BY TAX REFORM.

YES, WELL, THAT'S BECAUSE THEY NEED TO BE TOLD THAT TAX REFORM MEANS...

THIM

...A TAX CUT FOR YOU! MORE MONEY FOR YOU! YOU GOT THAT?

YEH, BUT WHAT ABOUT THE DEFICIT? HOW CAN I GET A TAX CUT IN THE MIDDLE OF A DEFICIT CRISIS...

...WHEN THEY'RE DISCUSSING DRASTIC MEASURES...

...TO CUT THE BUDGET, AND EMBARKING ON STAR WARS SPENDING,...

AND TALKING ABOUT THE NEED TO RAISE TAXES?

RATHER THAN GIVING ME MY MONEY AND THEN TAKING IT BACK AGAIN, WHY DON'T YOU JUST KEEP IT?

OH NO! NO! PLEASE TAKE A TAX CUT! PLEASE! PLEASE.

OH, ALL RIGHT.

WAIT! STOP! DON'T **DO** IT! YOU'LL CAUSE A RECESSION!

I GIVE UP!

NO! PLEASE! TAKE A TAX CUT! DON'T LISTEN TO HIM! DON'T LISTEN TO **HIM**!

(SIGH!)

MASTERS OF THE BUREAUCRAVERSE

©1985 m.a.s.

LIKE SO MANY OTHERS, HE HAD BEEN LURED FROM ANOTHER WORLD BY THE INTOXICATING GRAVITATIONAL POWER OF THE PLANET WASHINGTRON IN THE MIDDLE OF THE BELTY WAY.

I HAIL FROM THE PLANET FINANCIA. I SEEK THE POWERS OF WASHINGTRON.

FOR FOUR FRUSTRATING YEARS, HOWEVER, HE WAS FORCED TO ENDURE THE EQUALITY OF MANY OF HIS COLLEAGUES, HAUNTED ALL THE WHILE BY HIS SENSE OF SUPERIORITY.

WHEN WILL THE TRUTH BE REVEALED?

THEN ONE NIGHT HE HAD A DREAM IN WHICH HE SAW HIMSELF AS A POWERFUL GIANT, HOVERING OVER WASHINGTRON. BEHIND HIM WAS AN ENCHANTED DOOR.

SUDDENLY, HE AWOKE.

THAT DREAM!... IT FELT SO... SO REAL!

IN THE DARKNESS, A VISION APPEARED BEFORE HIM AND SPOKE.

I AM THE MOST IMPORTANT FORCE IN THE UNIVERSE: YOUR EGO.

...SOON THE DOOR IN THE DREAM WILL APPEAR TO YOU AND MAGIC WORDS WILL BE REVEALED IN YOUR MIND.

AND IT CAME TO PASS THAT HE BECAME WHITE HOUSE CHIEF OF STAFF AND WHENEVER ANYONE WANTED ACCESS TO THE OVAL OFFICE, HE WOULD SAY THE MAGIC WORDS:

ACCESS DENIED!

AND EACH TIME HE DID THIS HE GREW LARGER AND OTHER PEOPLE GREW SMALLER.

C-COULD YOU GIVE HIM A M-MES-SAGE?

BUT THERE WAS STILL ONE CREATURE IN WASHINGTRON THAT WOULD NOT SUCCUMB TO HIS WILL: THE 535-HEADED MONSTER KNOWN AS CONGRESSAURUS

NO YES NO YES MAYBE NO

FOR THAT HE HAD TO OPEN THE MAGIC DOOR AND RELEASE PRESIDENTRON.

HERE YA' GO, BOY! GOOD BOY!

CONGRESS CANDIES CANDIDATES LOVE 'EM!

THEY EAT RIGHT OUT OF HIS HAND!

TERRORIST MORNING NEWS

WELCOME TO THE "TERRORIST MORNING NEWS"...

I'M YOUR HOST MARTYR.

GOOD WARNING AMERICA

LATER IN THE PROGRAM WE WILL INTRODUCE OUR NEWEST HOSTAGES AND ANNOUNCE THE DEMANDS THAT MUST BE MET FOR THEIR RELEASE.

TERROR BROADCASTING NETWORK

BUT, FIRST, THE NEWS...

GOOD WARNING AMERICA

THERE WAS A SLOWDOWN IN TRADING THIS WEEK IN THE HOSTAGE MARKETS.

ANALYSTS ATTRIBUTE THIS TO A DECLINE IN THE SHOCK VALUE OF HOSTAGE SEIZURES DUE TO RECENT MARKET FLOODING.

AS A RESULT, LEADING MARTYR STRATEGISTS HAVE BEEN CALLING FOR THE ESTABLISMENT OF A TERROR CONTROL BOARD...

...TO REGULATE THE SHOCK VALUES OF TERRORIST INCIDENTS.

THEY FACE STRONG OPPOSITION, HOWEVER, FROM MARTYRS WHO BELIEVE THAT THIS WOULD VIOLATE THE SACRED PRINCIPLE OF FREE MARKET KIDNAPPING.

AND NOW FOR A LOOK AT SPORTS...

WITH EMBASSY-BOMBING SEASON ABOUT TO BEGIN, ALL EYES ARE ON A FEW LEADING COMPETITORS...

LET'S SEE NOW... POUR THE ELECTORATE INTO A BIG POT...

RECIPES

© 1986 M.A.S.

SEASON GENEROUSLY WITH ONLY THE MOST CAREFULLY SELECTED "FACTS."

STIR CHARISMATICALLY FOR WEEKS, MONTHS, YEARS...

WHEEEEE!!

THEN ADD YOUR FAVORITE POLICY MIX.

...UH-OH! RUNNING LOW!

LOW-TAX DEFENSE $ MIX FOR BALANCED BUDGET UPSIDE DOWN CAKE

RIDING HIGH, MEANWHILE, WERE SPIRITS AT THE ANNUAL CONVENTION OF THE ASSOCIATION FOR CORRECT BELIEFS.

THAT'S HARD TO BELIEVE.

OF COURSE. IT'S A MIRACLE.

HOW DID YOU FIND OUT?

IT'S IN THE SCRIPTURES. THE WHOLE STORY IS ON THESE CASSETTE TAPES.

THE LORD HAS BEEN A STRONG SUPPORTER OF THE STRATEGIC DEFENSE INITIATIVE FOR CENTURIES. IT WAS DESTINED.

HE ALSO FAVORS AID TO THE NICARAGUAN "FREEDOM FIGHTERS."

YOU CAN BE A

WHAT'S HIS POSITION ON GRAMM-RUDMAN?

WELL, ACTUALLY, THE CORRECT NAME FOR THAT BILL IS: "GRAMM-RUDMAN-HOLLINGS-GOD."

ONE NIGHT, AFTER SEVERAL DRINKS,...

I LIKE THE IDEA OF A DEFICIT REDUCTION AMENDMENT.

IT ALLOWS ME TO SAY: I DID BUT I DIDN'T.

ALL **I** DID WAS VOTE TO CUT THE **DEFICIT**! **NOT** THE BUDGET!

©1985 m.a.s.

...WHAT WE DID WAS: WE CREATED AN **INVISIBLE FORCE** THAT WILL ERADICATE THE DEFICIT IN THE **FUTURE**.

IF THAT FORCE CUTS ANY PROGRAMS THAT BENEFIT **YOU**,...WELL, PLEASE REMEMBER:...

...**I** WOULD **NOT** HAVE MADE THOSE CUTS. SO DON'T BLAME **ME**...

...BLAME THE INVISIBLE FORCE.

BOB ROSE TO HIS FEET UNSTEADILY AND MEANDERED INTO HIS OFFICE.

ONE ALERT AIDE MADE CAREFUL NOTES.

BOB WOULD APPRECIATE THIS LATER.

YOU'RE SERIOUS ABOUT THIS, AREN'T YOU BOB?

GINGER, IT'S WORKING ALREADY... LOOK! THERE I AM!...

THE TIME HAS COME...

..TO TAKE **IMMEDIATE ACTION** TO **SOLVE** OUR DEFICIT PROBLEM SOMETIME IN THE FUTURE!

A HOME RUN!, WOULDN'T YOU SAY, GINGER? ...JUST THINK HOW MANY PEOPLE ARE WATCHING THIS!

BOB, I DON'T GET IT...

SAID THE CONGRESS-MAN'S WIFE.

HOW IS THIS AMENDMENT GOING TO REDUCE THE DEFICIT IN THE FUTURE WHEN CONGRESS CAN'T AGREE ON ANY SPECIFIC WAY TO REDUCE IT RIGHT NOW?

I MEAN, IT JUST SEEMS SO... ABSTRACT!

EXACTLY! THAT'S THE POINT!

WHAT DO YOU MEAN?

WHILE IT'S TRUE THAT MANY PEOPLE ARE GETTING WORRIED ABOUT IT, THE FACT IS THAT, FOR MOST OF THEM, THE DEFICIT IS STILL, BASICALLY, AN ABSTRACTION...

...WHICH WE, THEREFORE, SOLVE WITH ANOTHER ABSTRACTION. THE LOGIC IS AIRTIGHT.

YES, BUT WHAT HAPPENS WHEN THINGS START BECOMING MORE... REAL?

IT'S REMARKS LIKE THAT, GINGER, THAT MAKE ME WONDER WHAT PLANET YOU'RE FROM.

IT WAS JUST A CRAZY THOUGHT.

SO, BOB,...SUPPOSE WE DEVELOP **S.D.I.** AND DEPLOY IT IN OUTER SPACE. EVEN ITS **PROPONENTS** ADMIT IT WON'T BE 100% EFFECTIVE.

© 1985 m.A.8

STRATEGIC DEFENSE INITIATIVE From The Possibilities OF SURVIVAL Strategic Defense Initiative

...WHAT HAPPENS WHEN THE SURVIVING MISSILES REACH THE EARTH? MILLIONS OF PEOPLE WILL BE KILLED!

NOT AT **ALL**, GINGER!

THERE ARE MANY PROPOSED SOLUTIONS FOR THAT VERY CONTINGENCY!

LIKE WHAT?

WELL, LIKE **THIS** ONE, FOR EXAMPLE..

STRATEGIC DEFENSE BUBBLE GUM

1045

AT THE FIRST SIGN OF A NUCLEAR ATTACK, A SPECIAL ALERT WILL BE SOUNDED.

THE CITIZENS WILL BE INSTRUCTED TO BLOW A BUBBLE.

ALL CITIZENS: COMMENCE DEPLOYMENT OF ANTI-MISSILE GUM!

ANY MISSILE PASSING THROUGH THE PEACE SHIELD WILL BE CAUGHT IN THE MAGNETIC PULSE EMITTED BY THE GUM.

..."WHEN THE MISSILE HITS THE BUBBLE, IT WILL BOUNCE ONCE...

..."THEN FALL TO EARTH WITH THE GUM STUCK TO ITS TIP. THE **GUM'S** MAGNETIC PULSE WILL DEACTIVATE THE WARHEAD, RENDERING IT HARMLESS."

BOB, THAT'S **CRAZY!** IT'S... **TOTALLY IMPOSSIBLE!**

THAT'S WHAT THEY SAID ABOUT THE AIRPLANE AT ONE TIME.

BUT, BOB...

PEOPLE THOUGHT THE WRIGHT BROTHERS WERE CRAZY!

BUT... IN 1899, THE HEAD OF THE U.S. PATENT OFFICE SAID "EVERYTHING THAT CAN BE INVENTED **HAS** BEEN INVENTED."

GEE...

WHAT WOULD HE HAVE THOUGHT OF SPACE TRAVEL?

GOSH.

JUST IMAGINE, GINGER, JUST FOR A MOMENT: A BUBBLE GUM THAT COULD PROTECT US FROM NUCLEAR MISSILES AND TASTES GOOD TOO!

WOW!

FIRST, THE BOLTING UPRIGHT, SUDDENLY, WITHOUT WARNING.

THEN THE EXTENSION OF HIS ARMS, INVOLUNTARILY THRUSTING FORWARD, HANDS GRASPING VAINLY AT THE TROPICAL AIR.

©1983 M.A.S.

AND THE BENDING OF HIS NECK, SLIGHTLY FORWARD, EYES OPENED WIDER, WIDER

ARE YOU ALL RIGHT, ARTHUR?

NEWSPAPER. GET ME A NEWSPAPER. NEWSPAPER! NEWSPAPER...

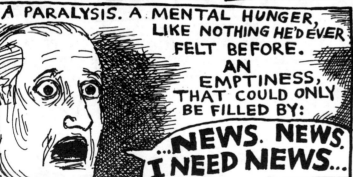

A PARALYSIS. A MENTAL HUNGER, LIKE NOTHING HE'D EVER FELT BEFORE. AN EMPTINESS, THAT COULD ONLY BE FILLED BY:

...NEWS. NEWS. I NEED NEWS...

SUCH WERE THE SYMPTOMS OF "NEWS ADDICTION REFLEX", SCOURGE OF MANY VACATIONING WASHINGTONIANS, WHO, ANXIOUS TO "GET AWAY FROM IT ALL", GOT TOO FAR AWAY TOO FAST.

HERE, DEAR. I FOUND A NEWSPAPER IN THE HOTEL.

...NEWS... NEWS...

ONE BIT OF NEWS NOT REPORTED IN THAT NEWSPAPER WAS THE CONTINUING FAILURE OF THE PULVEREX WEAPONS SYSTEM.

A BILLION OR TWO MORE AND WE'LL HAVE THE KINKS WORKED OUT.

AND PART OF THOSE BILLIONS WAS HEADED FOR BOB FOREHEAD'S CONGRESSIONAL DISTRICT.

AND ANOTHER PART WAS HEADED FOR HIS CAMPAIGN FUND.

...THE PULVEREX IS CRITICAL TO OUR NATION'S DEFENSE!...

THEY LET HIM BRING HIS PIANO TO THE MISSILE-TESTING RANGE.

HE LIKED TO GET CLOSE TO HIS SUBJECT.

©1983 M.A.S.

THE CHIEF ENGINEER FOR THE MISSILE WAS THERE ALSO, ...and VERY CONCERNED.

WE WANT YOU TO CAPTURE the ESSENTIAL **PERSONALITY** OF OUR MISSILE... ITS GRACE, ...ITS COY ELUSIVENESS, ...THE ELOQUENCE OF ITS DESTRUCTIVE POWER!

IN MUSIC SCHOOL, HE'D NEVER IMAGINED HIMSELF COMPOSING BACKGROUND MUSIC FOR A PROMOTIONAL FILM ABOUT THE "CRAZE MISSILE," BUT IT BEAT WAITING ON TABLES.

MORE GRANDEUR! ... MORE ROMANCE! ...

ALL OF THEM WERE GLAD TO BE WORKING: THE CINEMATOGRAPHERS, THE **PHOTO**GRAPHERS, THE WRITERS, THE DESIGNERS OF THE BROCHURE, ...

IF THEY DID A GOOD JOB ON THIS ONE, THEY **MIGHT** HAVE A CHANCE TO MAKE PROMO-TIONAL MATERIAL FOR WEAPONS OF **ULTIMATE** DESTRUCTION, WHICH PAID A LOT MORE...

TIME-ENDER MISSILE

DISASTER MASTER

PULVEREX

GETS THE JOB DONE FAST!

..FEW PEOPLE REALIZE THE GREAT CONTRIBUTION THAT THE ARMS RACE HAS MADE TO THE ARTS...

SAID CONGRESSMAN BOB FOREHEAD, SPEAKING TO AN ARTS SOCIETY IN HIS HOME DISTRICT.

EVERY YEAR, HUNDREDS OF CREATIVE TALENTS ARE EMPLOYED AND GIVEN INVAL-UABLE EXPERIENCE PUTTING TOGETHER THE ANNUAL WEAPONS FESTIVAL IN WASHINGTON, D.C.

...THE RESULT IS AN EXPERIENCE I WISH I COULD SHARE WITH YOU ALL...

HE SHOULD HAVE KNOWN BETTER THAN TO WALK IN THAT NEIGHBORHOOD AT THAT TIME OF NIGHT.

AT QUARTER TO SEVEN, THE FIRST ONE APPEARED.

GOOD EVENING.

HE TRIED TO IGNORE HIM, BUT THE MAN FOLLOWED HIM.

©1986 m.a.b.

SOON ANOTHER APPEARED, AND ANOTHER, AND ANOTHER... IN TWOS, IN THREES... GATHERING OMINOUSLY AROUND HIM...

SUDDENLY, AT SEVEN, THEY CLOSED IN. HE WAS SURROUNDED. HE DIDN'T HAVE A CHANCE.

GOOD EVENING. IT'S TIME FOR THE...

...EVENING NEWS.

NO-O-O! NOT THAT! NOT AGAIN!

WITH WILD ABANDON, THE MOB OF CRAZED ANCHORPERSONS CARRIED HIM AWAY TO THEIR STUDIO HIDE-OUT AND BEGAN INFORMING HIM OF THE NEWS OF THE DAY.

...THE DOLLAR IS...

NO! STOP IT! I DON'T WANT TO HEAR IT!

...DOWN 30% SINCE...

THE NEWS ANCHOR BUSINESS WAS FIERCELY COMPETITIVE. FOR EVERY "DAN", "TOM", "PETER", OR "TED", THERE WERE TENS OF THOUSANDS OF FRUSTRATED, UNEMPLOYED, WOULD-BE ANCHORPERSONS RUNNING LOOSE IN AMERICA'S STREETS...

SO, WHOM SHOULD WE INFORM TONIGHT?

...VIOLATING THE FREEDOM OF IGNORANCE OF FELLOW CITIZENS.

IN THE ILLINOIS PRIMARY,...

DON'T TELL ME! I'M BORED! LET'S TALK ABOUT SPORTS...

IT WAS RAPIDLY BECOMING A MAJOR SOCIAL MENACE. THE REIGNING ANCHORPERSONS TRIED TO WARN AMERICA.

IF YOUR CHILD SHOWS ANY OF THE SEVEN DANGER SIGNS OF ANCHORPERSONISM, REMEMBER: I WON'T RETIRE UNTIL 2007.

HEY, MOM, WHERE'S THE BLOWDRYER?

PULVEREX

I WANT TO MAKE IT CLEAR, ONCE AND FOR ALL, THAT **I AM SINCERE** IN MY CONCERN ABOUT GENDER GAPS ...I MEAN, **SWING VOTES** ...I MEAN, UH, WOMEN'S ...UH...RIGHTS!

Said the PRESIDENT. BUT HIS WORDS WERE NOT WELL-RECEIVED,

...WHICH WAS SIMILAR TO THE EXPERIENCE OF A PARTICULAR MUSICIAN IN HIS EARLY ATTEMPTS AT COMPOSING BACKGROUND MUSIC FOR A PROMOTIONAL FILM ABOUT the CRAZE MISSILE.

plinkadinkatinka...

NO NO! THAT'S NOT IT! NOT AT ALL!... SAID THE ENGINEERS OF THE MISSILE.

©1983 m.A.&

...I DON'T GET THE FEELING THAT YOU REALLY **CARE** ABOUT OUR MISSILE! THERE'S A LACK OF SENSITIVITY...

THEY'D BEEN THROUGH SO MUCH TOGETHER, THESE ENGINEERS. THEY'D **SHARED** SO MUCH: THE STRUGGLE, THE VICTORIES... LIKE THE DAY THEY FINALLY SUCCEEDED AT DOUBLING THEIR MISSILE'S KILL RATIO.

...I DON'T THINK YOU REALIZE HOW MUCH **LOVE** HAS GONE INTO THE DEVELOPMENT OF THIS WEAPON!

MULTIPLY THAT LOVE MANY TIMES AND YOU GET SOME IDEA OF THE EMOTION GENERATED BY THE **PULVEREX** WEAPONS SYSTEM, PROVIDER OF JOBS, CREATOR OF ENTIRE COMMUNITIES...

GLOMINOID, INC.

ARMAGEDDON ESTATES

AT THE ANNUAL WEAPONS FESTIVAL in WASHINGTON, THE PULVEREX WOULD HAVE ONE OF THE LARGEST BOOTHS.

PULVEREX
PEACE THROUGH MASS-ANNIHILATIVE INSTANTANEOUSNESS

JUGGLERS, PUPPETEERS, AND FASHION MODELS WOULD BE THERE TO DEMONSTRATE ITS AWESOME DESTRUCTIVE POWER.

HI, FOLKS!

...AND CONGRESSMAN FOREHEAD WOULD BE THERE TOO.

PULVEREX

BOMBS   MISSILES   FIGHTER PLANES

OH BOY! OH BOY!

A SMALL CLUMP OF EARTH, PACKED *together* to just A CERTAIN DENSITY.

Bulldozers *made* the BEST ONES WHEN DIGGING THE FOUNDATION FOR a NEW HOUSE.

Kids CALLED *them* "DIRT BOMBS."

GOTCHA!

©1983 M.A.S.

THEY WERE STEVEN'S FIRST EXPERIENCE WITH "EXPLOSIVES." HE WAS 5, and FASCINATED.

IN HIGH SCHOOL, HE WAS ONE OF THOSE GUYS YOU MIGHT HAVE SAT NEXT to IN ALGEBRA, WHO WAS ALWAYS DRAWING PICTURES OF *machine-like* THINGS... AIRPLANES, ROCKETS ... VERY *intensely.*

HE WAS NEVER MUCH INTERESTED *in* SPORTS, EXCEPT FOR ONE: NUCLEAR ARMS RACING

SPORTS
RUSSIA TIES U.S. IN MISSILES
LIZ RE-MARRIES
NEW PRE DEN

HE WANTED to BE ON the TEAM.

KILTEK CORPORATION

YOU'RE HIRED!

PERSONNEL

HE WORKED AS AN ENGINEER. HE WAS BRILLIANT, INITIATING DEVELOPMENT OF THE "NERVOUSNESS MISSILE," A SPECTACULAR TECHNOLOGICAL BREAKTHROUGH.

FAST, ACCURATE, and DEADLY, THIS MISSILE COULD LAUNCH AUTOMATICALLY WHEN TRIGGERED BY THE SENSING OF HUMAN NERVOUSNESS *within* A ONE-MILE RADIUS.

THUS, AT LAST, the MERE FEAR OF ATTACK COULD LAUNCH *an* INSTANT COUNTER-ATTACK.

DEPLOYMENT OF THIS MISSILE COULD GREATLY ACCELERATE the DESTABILIZATION OF U.S.-SOVIET RELATIONS...

SAID A DEFENSE STOCK ANALYST *to* A ROOMFUL OF INVESTORS.

...THUS CAUSING A DRAMATIC RISE IN THE VALUE OF DEFENSE-RELATED STOCKS..

..(PRECEDED BY A DRAMATIC RISE IN MANY CONGRESSMEN'S CAMPAIGN FUNDS.)

WE NEED THAT MISSILE, BOB!

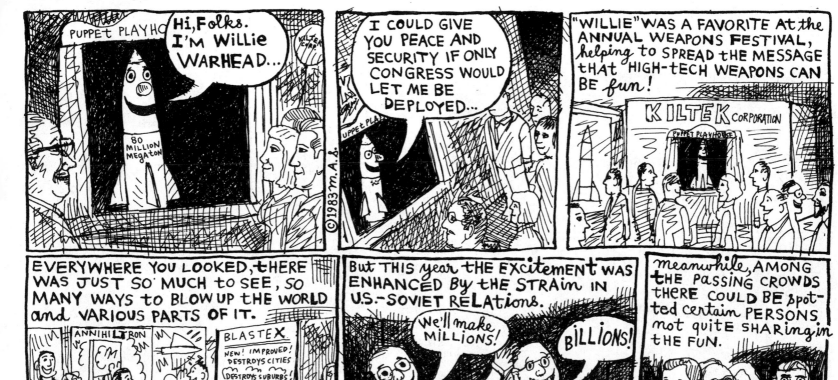

MANY ADULTS WERE QUITE DISTURBED BY THE TESTIMONY OF *children* AT A *congressional* HEARING.

...I GET SO SCARED OF A NUCLEAR WAR. SO MANY COUNTRIES HAVE NUCLEAR WEAPONS. I WISH NOBODY HAD ANY!

AMONG *those* MOST DISTURBED, WERE OFFICIALS at the DEPARTMENT OF DEFENSE.

THIS IS **TERRIBLE!** ...JUST **TERRIBLE!** ...to HAVE **LITTLE CHILDREN** LIVING *in* **FEAR** OF **NUCLEAR WEAPONS!**...

©1983 M.A.S.

...IT'S A THREAT to the FUTURE OF the ARMS RACE!

WE'VE GOT to DO SOMETHING TO TURN THIS AROUND BEFORE WE RAISE A *Generation* OF **SISSIES!**

I'D SAY IT'S A PROBLEM OF EDUCATION.

I'VE GOT AN IDEA!

SAID A STAFFER *recalling* THE KILTEK EXHIBIT at the ANNUAL WEAPONS FESTIVAL.

KILTEK CORPORATION

HI! I'M WILLIE WARHEAD!

WILLIE WARHEAD HAS *the* POTENTIAL TO WIELD *enormous* INFLUENCE AMONG CHILDREN. IF PROPERLY MARKETED, HE COULD BE *the* NEXT SNOOPY!

From *there,* THE IDEA TOOK OFF. A T.V. PRODUCTION COMPANY *was* CONTACTED.

SEVERAL MONTHS LATER *the* SHOW WENT ON THE AIR *and* EVERY SATURDAY MORNING *millions* OF YOUNGSTERS *could* WATCH:

...THE WILLIE WARHEAD CARTOON SHOW!

EACH WEEK WILLIE'S PAL, SAM, WOULD BE THREATENED BY A BIG BAD BEAR FROM *the* "EVIL EMPIRE!"

THEN SAM WOULD RUN TO CONGRESS *and* BEG THEM TO DEPLOY WILLIE.

PLEASE! BEFORE IT'S TOO LATE!

BUT CONGRESS WOULD REFUSE!

THEN SAM WOULD TURN TO THE KIDS AT HOME...

YOU'VE GOT TO HELP ME, KIDS!

...and HE'D LEAD THEM IN A ROUSING CHANT:

DEPLOY WILLIE! DEPLOY WILLIE! DEPLOY WILLIE!...

FINALLY, CONGRESS WOULD GIVE *in* AND WILLIE WOULD DETER THE EVIL BEAR ONCE AGAIN.

YA-A-A-AY WILLIE!!

THEY WERE SHOWING UP WITH INCREASING FREQUENCY in CONGRESSMAN BOB FOREHEAD'S MAIL.

I THOUGHT YOU'D LIKE TO SEE THESE. ...THEY'RE CUTE.

SAID BOB.

©1983 M.A.B.

THAT WILLIE WARHEAD IS REALLY DOING HIS JOB!

said A LOBBYIST from the KILTEK CORPORATION.

and QUITE A BIG JOB IT WAS.

...REMEMBER, KIDS, THE THREE KEYS TO GOOD HEALTH ARE: PLENTY OF EXERCISE, A BALANCED DIET,...

80 MILLION MEGATON

...AND A STRONG NUCLEAR DETERRENT!

ANYTHING YOU SAY, WILLIE!

Included in WILLIE'S "BALANCED DIET" were two BRAND new cereals:

SUGAR NUKES

THE CANDY-COATED CEREAL IN THE SHAPE OF YOUR FAVORITE NUCLEAR WEAPONS!

and:

NEUTRON CRISPIES

the CEREAL THAT EXPLODES IN MILK WITHOUT BREAKING THE BOWL.

BOOOM!

ON WEEKENDS, WILLIE VISITED SHOPPING MALLS ALL across THE COUNTRY, PROMOTING WILLIE WARHEAD TOYS and OTHER PRODUCTS.

WILLIE WARHEAD BUBBLE GUM TRADING CARDS

WILLIE WARHEAD JOGGING SHOES FOR TOTS

WILLIE WARHEAD LUNCHBOX

WILLIE WARHEAD BOARD GAME

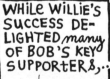

WHILE WILLIE'S SUCCESS DELIGHTED many OF BOB'S KEY SUPPORTERS,...

IT HAD A DIFFERENT EFFECT ON A A KEY MEMBER OF HIS FAMILY.

A LITTLE MORE BOUNCE in HIS STEP, a little more SELF-ASSURANCE.

...U.S. Marines have taken Grenada...

I JUST FEEL BETTER. IT'S AN OVERALL FEELING, A SENSE OF WELL-BEING.

© 1983 M.A.S.

HE WASN'T the ONLY ONE. LOTS OF AMERICANS were FEELING IT.

WE'VE Finally ASSERTED OURSELVES.

NOW THE WORLD KNOWS WE can't BE PUSHED AROUND!

GOSH! IF A small-scale INVASION FEELS THIS GOOD, IMAGINE HOW GREAT A WAR WOULD FEEL!

meanwhile, EXHAUSTIVE OPINION POLLS WERE BEING taken.

IF U.S. MARINES INVADED NICARAGUA AND THE ENSUING CONFLICT WERE MADE INTO A TV MINI-SERIES, WOULD YOU WATCH IT?

YES.

SAID 62 PERCENT.

meanwhile, IN Congressman BOB FOREHEAD'S OFFICE, HIS STAFF WAS FEEDING RESULTS OF these POLLS into their new COMPUTER.

THEN THEY WAITED FOR BOB'S NEWEST POSITIONS TO BE PRINTED OUT.

HOW DO I FEEL ABOUT LEBANON?

ASKED BOB.

THE COMPUTER RESPONDED WITH A STREAM OF DARK SMOKE.

It seems to be breaking down.

FOR A BRIEF moment BOB WAS AFRAID. HOW COULD HE FACE THE PRESS?

Then HE REMEMBERED the WORDS OF HIS CHARISMATICIAN:

WHEN the going GETS TOUGH, the TOUGH LEARN TO FAKE IT.

BOB HELD A PRESS CONFERENCE THAT DAY AND HANDLED IT SO WELL THAT NOBODY HAD ANY IDEA WHERE HE STOOD ON ANYTHING.

NBP IS A COMMON CONDITION AFFECTING THE VAST MAJORITY OF HUMAN BEINGS. MOST OF US LEARN TO ACCEPT IT AND COPE WITH IT.

explained THE DOCTOR to GINGER FOREHEAD WHEN SHE ARRIVED *at* THE HOSPITAL.

© 1985 m.a.l.

THERE ARE SOME PEOPLE, *however*, LIKE YOUR HUSBAND, WHOSE *chemical* MAKEUP SUBJECTS *them* TO PERIODIC, AND SOMETIMES VOLATILE, **NBP** REACTIONS.

WHAT IS "NBP"?

"NOT BEING PRESIDENT."

CAN I SEE HIM?

...UH,... NOT JUST YET. HE'S...UH ...RESTING.

THE DOCTOR FELT BOB WASN'T READY FOR VISITORS.

...ELECT ME! ELECT ME!

CALM DOWN, MR. FOREHEAD.

HE WAS SO UPSET THAT HE EVEN MISSED HIS FAVORITE TV SHOW:

THE McLAUGH-IN GROUP
VOLUME V NO. XLIII — WEEKEND EDITION
LIBERALISM IS DEAD

ISSUE ONE: LIBERALISM IS COMPLETELY WASHED UP. THE DEMOCRATIC PARTY IS CRUMBLING AS WE SPEAK. LET'S HAVE A EULOGY. R. NOVANS?

WELL, FIRST OF *all*, JOHN, THE DEMOCRATS NEVER UNDERSTOOD THAT **NO ONE** OUTSIDE OF THE WASHINGTON BELTWAY HAS ANY INTEREST AT ALL IN BORING ISSUES LIKE TOXIC WASTE AND THE DEFICIT. VOTERS WANT FEEL-GOOD ISSUES LIKE TAX CUTS AND THE ARMS BUILDUP.

HA! HA! NOVANS HAS OUTDONE HIMSELF! THAT IS THE MOST RIDICULOUS THING HE'S EVER SAID, EXCEPT FOR ALMOST EVERYTHING **ELSE** HE'S EVER SAID!

IT'S NOT AS RIDICULOUS AS WHAT **YOU** JUST SAID!

WHAT **YOU** JUST SAID IS TOTALLY **IDIOTIC!**

FINALLY, THE MODERATOR INTERVENED.

YOU'RE **ALL** WRONG! I'M RIGHT. **ISSUE TWO**...

IT WAS NEWS-TALK'S ANSWER TO "THE HONEYMOONERS." A VIDEO NARCOTIC FOR POLITICAL JUNKIES. EVEN GINGER WAS HOOKED.

ISSUE 7

Hey, Sue. ...LET'S GET **SCARED** OF the SANDINISTAS. IT'S THE LATEST!

I'LL *tell* YOU WHAT *concerns* ME ABOUT *that:* ...I'M AFRAID *that* IF THE SIXTIES COME BACK IN THE LATE EIGHTIES, WE WOULD BE **TOTALLY** OUT OF STEP!

©1986 M.a.S.

THE SIXTIES **ARE** *coming* BACK, YES. ...THE **EARLY** SIXTIES! A TIME OF BOLD PATRIOTISM.

BUT **THIS** TIME WE WILL HAVE LEARNED FROM OUR MISTAKES AND WE WILL FIGHT TO **WIN!**

and **THEN** WHAT WILL HAPPEN IS WHAT **SHOULD HAVE** HAPPENED IN THE LATE SIXTIES: THE RETURN OF THE MID-FORTIES!

VICTORIOUS IN THE NICARAGUAN WAR, WE WILL **ONCE AGAIN** BE **FULLY** RESPECTED AS LEADERS OF THE FREE WORLD!

BUT *the* COUNTRY IS DIVIDED NOW. EVEN SUPPORT *for the* CONTRAS IS WEAK.

NOW, MORE *than* EVER, LET US HEED *the* ADVICE OF FRANKLIN ROOSEVELT! ...LET US **NOT** FEAR FEAR!

LET US **THRIVE** ON IT! LET US WORK OURSELVES *into* A FRENZY!...

and LOSE CONTROL OF OUR SENSES AND JUST GO WILD!

...OOH, YEH!... WOW! SOUNDS LIKE FUN!